Anyone Can Homeschool

How to Find What Works for You

by *Terry Dorian, Ph.D.*
and
Zan Peters Tyler

Huntington House Publishers

Huntington House Publishers
P.O. Box 53788
Lafayette, Louisiana 70505

Library of Congress Card Catalog Number 95-076166
ISBN 1-56384-095-2

Printed in the U.S.A.

Dedication of Part I
from Zan Peters Tyler

To Daddy, who gave me vision and a sense of destiny and taught me to embrace the impossible as just another challenge.

To Mother, whose patience and dedication taught me more about teaching than any university ever could.

To my sister Donna, whose character has encouraged and challenged me, even though I'll never measure up!

And, to my sister Sybil, who was my first homeschooling project. May God bless you for the load you had to bear!

Dedication of Part II
from Terry Dorian

To my dear husband, Gary—whose strength and faithfulness in Christ have transformed my life. To our children—Jessica, Cannaan, Christian, and Jenna—whose love, joy, kindness and mercy bless us every day of our lives. And to our married children—Kimberly and Darren Lancaster; and Stacey and Patrick Dee—whose love for the Lord encourages our hearts. And to my wonderful Mother, Elouise C. Hicks, and my precious, Dad, the late Wiley H. Hicks—whose love and generosity opened worlds for me. And to our children's children.

What Others Have Said about *Anyone Can Homeschool*:

"Tyler and Terry Dorian offer a concise and comprehensible examination of the philosophical choices and practical challenges which all of us face as home-educating parents. Their insights are both unique and compelling. Zan and Terry demystify the process of homeschooling and empower the reader. They inspire our confidence in the ability of ordinary parents to accomplish amazing things."

—Michael P. Farris,
president and founder of
Home School Legal Defense Association

"*Anyone Can Homeschool* promises to become the standard handbook for parents to find out what works in quality Christian homeschooling."

—D. James Kennedy, Ph.D., Coral Ridge
Presbyterian Church; President,
Evangelism Explosion International

Contents

——————— **Appendices** ———————

Foreword

Anyone Can Homeschool, How to Find What Works for You is neither a how-to book, offering daily schedules and chore charts, nor a resource guide, summarizing the instructional methods and materials which are available. Instead, the authors offer a clear, concise, and eminently readable book that explains both the process of homeschooling, as well as the educational philosophies that have impacted the home education movement. Their orientation tour is not only delightful, it is compelling and challenging, as well.

In the course of our ministry, my wife, Nancy, and I meet thousands of home educators. Each summer we have the privilege of sharing the Word in song with our precious friends at Bill Gothard's Advanced Training Institute held in Knoxville, Tennessee. We recognize the worth of homeschooling because we know homeschooling families. We see what happens when parents and children are committed to biblical principles. Not only do their lives change, their churches, their communities—and even the various countries they visit—change as they share their lives in Christ.

The psalmist speaks of having the soul of a weaned child, composed and quieted. He describes the person who has a childlike trust in the Lord as one "whose heart is not proud, nor eyes haughty." This is the heart and soul that I see reflected in *Anyone Can Homeschool*. The authors are women of the Word who "smile at the future" and who "open their mouths in wisdom." "The teaching of kindness" is on their tongues (Prov. 25:25, 26).

Many of the home educators whom we know and love are confounded by the world of curriculum fairs and manuals, instructional resources and materials, homeschooling catalogues and resource guides. They need guidance in order to make sense of all that information. I believe that *Anyone Can Homeschool* will meet their needs by leading them through the maze of contradictory ideas and theories. Readers everywhere who have been inundated with advice and options will gain a liberating perspective when they read this book.

The Lord has gifted the authors and trained them by His Spirit. They have found their identity in Him, and they have found Him faithful in the fires of affliction. I know Joe and Zan Tyler by reputation. They are faithful servants of the Lord. They serve their local community, their state, and country as leaders in the home education movement. Zan's keen insights into why homeschooling works and her understanding of sanctification in the homeschooling process have touched our hearts. I believe her words will encourage and challenge every reader.

Gary and Terry Dorian and their children are our close personal friends. We are intimately acquainted with the major and minor events in each other's lives. The parting of the Red Sea, Paul's experience on the road to Damascus, blind Bartimaeus, and the woman who touched the hem of His garment are realities in their lives. They know the God of miracles and grace, and they serve Him. Terry is a gifted teacher, who is able to make complex ideas immediately comprehensible to the reader. That is a spiritual gift. Her words help us to renew our vision and motivate us to make ourselves available to God.

Those readers who have enjoyed homeschooling for decades; those who are just beginning to homeschool; and those who would simply like to gain insight into the heart and soul of the home education movement will find this book indispensable.

The unfolding of Thy words gives light;
It gives understanding to the simple. (Ps.119:130)

May God richly bless you!
"Sing"cerely yours,

ALFRED B. SMITH

Part I

by Zan Peters Tyler

Anyone Can Homeschool

Anyone can homeschool. What a bold statement! I can see the raised eyebrows and feel the skepticism. I began homeschooling over a decade ago with great fear, hesitation, and trepidation. I wasn't sure that anyone *should*, much less *could*, homeschool. Twelve years later, here I am, shouting for the world to hear, "Anyone can homeschool—including you!"

What accounts for my 180 degree change in attitude? The answer lies in spending thousands of hours in research, meeting with countless homeschooling parents, and spending a delightfully life-changing decade teaching my own children.

Any student of logic knows that most sweeping generalizations cannot stand without qualification. Must the statement *anyone can homeschool* be qualified? Probably—but in a much different way than your common sense may dictate. The qualifying ingredient is not educational credentials or socioeconomic standing—the qualifying ingredient is motivation. Anyone who wants to homeschool can.

Like other things in life, motivation and commitment are the primary indicators of success. An unfaltering commitment to your child's welfare will enable you to view hindrances as challenges, rather than barriers, and allow you to creatively persevere in the pursuit of family-centered education.

Recently, I spent the afternoon at the State House lobbying for some homeschooling legislation. I came home tired and discouraged. I had no inclination to answer the phone as I walked in the door until I heard the voice on my answering machine. "Zan, this is Faye. I'm home from California for a week and I want to homeschool. Will you please call me?"

I reached for the phone, relieved to speak with a friendly voice from the past. Faye and I had graduated from Furman University together in 1977. She was the only graduate to receive a standing ovation. She later attended a seminary and received her master's degree in church music, graduating as the outstanding music student. She has the voice of an angel and pursued a professional singing career until she married and had children. And now, she wants to homeschool. Amazing—you see, Faye has been totally blind since birth. She has raised her three-and five-year-old boys without any help, except from her husband. She refuses to be discouraged by the obstacles in her life and perseveres with a tenacity that puts most of us to shame. To overcome her biggest barrier, she has purchased a computer equipped with the capacity to "read." She has researched curriculum choices and the law and is ready to begin. Anyone who wants to homeschool can.

Steve and Mamie decided to homeschool their eight children four years ago, pulling five of them out of school. This would be a daunting task under the best of circumstances. Add to the equation a child who has been a total invalid since birth. Steve and Mamie and the children have cared for Kres at home, refusing to institutionalize him. Steve rearranged his work schedule to allow him to homeschool the three students in grades seven and above. As a pediatric surgeon, he began his day at 5:30 A.M. and completed surgery by 10:30 A.M. He scheduled office hours for 2:30 to 6:30 P.M., freeing the hours in between to be home and teach. Mamie cares for the preschoolers and teaches the elementary-age children, and together they all cared for Kres until he went home to be with the Lord last year. Anyone who wants to homeschool can.

Elise simply couldn't afford to homeschool her four girls anymore, but she refused to give up. She found a technician's job in a local hospital and began working the night-shift, 11:00 P.M. until 7:00 A.M. She would arrive home before her husband left for work and would homeschool the girls in the morning. She would sleep a little in the afternoons and leave for work after a family dinner. Elise kept up this grueling schedule for over two years. Now her two oldest girls are attending college on full scholarships, and Elise is the director of the High School Program for the South Carolina Association of Independent Home Schools (SCAIHS). Anyone who wants to homeschool can.

While they all faced difficult circumstances, Faye, Steve and Mamie, and Elise are all highly educated people. What about the person who does not have a college diploma? Belinda and Frank Hardy, both high school graduates, are doing a great job homeschooling their children. However, when we first received their application to homeschool, the SCAIHS staff reviewed it and turned it down. The mother had a difficult time completing the application; therefore, we were concerned about her being adequately equipped to teach her children. These parents simply would not take no for an answer. They have a son who is learning disabled, scoring very poorly on standardized tests, but receiving A's and B's on his report card in school. They were worried about his being promoted to second grade without an adequate foundation. They also have an older daughter who seemed to be "falling through the cracks." The Hardys drove several hours to the SCAIHS office to meet with our staff even though they could not afford the trip.

We finally agreed to accept the Hardys' application on the condition that the mother would work with the tutor they had hired to help the children. All have prospered under this arrangement. Homeschooling is ben-

efiting not only the basic skills of the children, but of the
mother as well.

The overwhelming majority of homeschooling parents are very literate, but even the most literate parents
have areas of weakness. While we should all work at self-
improvement, one of the beauties of homeschooling is
that our children need not be limited nor condemned by
our shortcomings. At one point in South Carolina's history, parents without college degrees were required to
make a passing score on the Education Entrance Examination (EEE) in order to be allowed to homeschool. The
EEE is a state-developed exam that must be passed by
those seeking a career in the teaching profession; it is
most often administered to juniors in college. The EEE
has three parts: reading, mathematics, and composition.
When one homeschooling mother took this test, she passed
the reading and composition sections, but failed the math.
Her daughter had recently taken the state basic skills test
for her grade level and achieved a perfect score on the
math section! Our children are not restricted by our limitations. In many instances we serve as facilitators and
coordinators while we watch our children surpass us.

I used to believe that the growth of the homeschooling
movement would be limited by the number of families
that depend on two incomes for survival or desired
lifestyles. While finances are definitely a limiting factor
for some, many parents are finding creative ways to meet
both the financial and educational challenges of
homeschooling. Many families are simply redefining their
lifestyles and learning to live on less. Others meet the
same challenge by setting up home offices. With the advent of computer technology, fax machines, and cellular
phones, many parents are bringing their offices home.
The combination of flexible work schedules and school
schedules allows many to homeschool who once thought
it financially impossible.

Many missionaries, pastors, other full-time Christian
workers, and seminary students choose to homeschool. I

have witnessed the lives of many students at Columbia International University (formerly Columbia Bible College) who have decided to homeschool in spite of overwhelmingly difficult financial situations. I have been inspired over the years by watching these families trust in God to meet their financial needs. Anyone who wants to homeschool must indeed count the costs; but, in the counting, don't forget we serve the One who owns the cattle on a thousand hills.

If I had a dollar for everyone who has said to me, "Oh, I could never homeschool," I would be a rich woman today. What some people really mean is that they *would* never do that. Others simply mean they think they could never homeschool; they are intimidated by the entire concept. From the outside looking in, homeschooling appears to be much more overwhelming than it actually is. Many suffer from the fear of the unknown. After all, most of us have no experiential knowledge of homeschooling; we attended traditional schools.

In the following eight chapters, we want to help you understand what homeschooling really is, so you can make the choice that's right for you and your family. We want to help you meet the challenges of homeschooling and embrace, rather than fear, the changes that you will inevitably need to make.

Chapter One

Why Would I Want to Homeschool?

The 1828 edition of Noah Webster's *An American Dictionary of the English Language* gives us this definition of *education*:

> **Education**, n. [L. educatio] The bringing up, as of a child; instruction; formation of manners. Education comprehends all that series of instruction and discipline which is intended to enlighten the understanding, correct the temper, and form the manners and habits of youth, and fit them for usefulness in their future stations. To give children a good education in manners, arts, and science is important; to give them a religious education is indispensable; and an immense responsibility rests on parents and guardians who neglect these duties.[1]

In 1984, my husband, Joe, and I were faced with making the decision between public and Christian school for my oldest son, who was then turning six. He has always been bright, gregarious, energetic, and challenging. His kindergarten experience should have been delightful. He was attending a church school with eight children, a wonderful teacher, and a center-oriented classroom. They were beginning reading, and by February, Ty was the only child not reading well. I watched as his extroverted personality began the metamorphosis into introversion. I knew I had to do something to "rescue"

my child; I just didn't know what. I pulled him out of
school in February with the intention of holding him back
a year and allowing him to repeat K-5, enabling him to
be at his prime, rather than behind, when he began first
grade. Within weeks, his vitality and love of life had returned; I had my son back.

Having made the decision to wait a year to enroll Ty
in first grade, Joe and I were faced with the challenge of
deciding where to enroll Ty in school. Our church had
established an elementary school program to expand on
their existing preschool and kindergarten program. (Ty
had been enrolled in another church school heretofore.)
For the first time, we were faced with the heart-rending
process of deciding between public education and Christian education. We supported our church and session as
they voted to expand the kindergarten program into a
school. We also wanted to be supportive of public education. When Joe and I moved back to South Carolina after
spending two years in Philadelphia and Boston, we bought
our house because it was located in the school district
where I had attended high school—a school district with
an excellent reputation. My sisters and I had all attended
public schools, my mother had taught in public schools,
and my father's uncle was a superintendent of schools in
a South Carolina school district.

We prayed and agonized over where to put Ty in
school. We were at a crossroads in his little life, and I felt
like I was faced with a lose-lose situation. At that point in
time, our church school was using a curriculum with little
use for the concept of readiness, and I knew if Ty were
exposed to a grueling year of academics, it could be his
undoing. The public school seemed to have a better grasp
of what five-year-olds needed, but could not share or
affirm our Christian world-and-life view. In the Christian
school, his world-and-life view would remain intact, while
his confidence and joy would be crushed by academic
pressure for which he was not ready.

In the midst of this agonizing process, which seemed

to last a millennium, I poured out my soul to a dear friend at one of our weekly Bible study and prayer sessions. I was twenty-eight with two sons, ages five and three; Susan was thirty-eight with one very quiet three-year-old son. She also held a masters degree in education and had taught in public schools. As I laid before her my choices for Ty and asked her to pray for Joe and me, she very quietly told me of her intentions to homeschool her son.

I will never forget the first time I heard that word—*homeschool!* The walls of Susan's little mobile home (they were seminary students preparing for the mission field) began to close in on me. My head was spinning, and I felt trapped. I graciously took the literature Susan offered me and ran out the door. I knew I would never homeschool.

On the way home, before even reading the literature, I began telling God and myself why I would never homeschool. Hadn't I already given up enough to be a stay-at-home mother? Besides, I had never wanted to teach and knew little about it. Mainly, homeschooling was absolutely the strangest thing I had ever heard of. My husband and I had gone through a semicult experience in college. For five years, I had been telling God I just wanted a normal, quiet life.

And now God was invading my life again with this idea of homeschooling. Along with some short studies, Susan gave me a copy of Dr. Raymond Moore's *Home Grown Kids*. Very reluctantly, I picked up the book and began to read. In spite of wanting to totally dismiss the idea of home education from my mind, I found myself increasingly fascinated by the principles espoused by Dr. and Mrs. Moore. Now I was truly in a quandary. I wanted to narrow my options for Ty, but found the field broadened instead to three choices—public, private, and home.

When the boys were young, I used my early morning walks as a time to clear my mind, meditate on Scripture, and pray. During one of those walks, I came to grips with what I had been denying for weeks: God was leading me to homeschool. To appreciate the anguish I was in, you must remember that I knew no one—not one person—who was actually homeschooling. *Homeschooling* was not a household word, as it is today. As I walked, I told the Lord that I was sorry, but I just could not homeschool. To this day I can remember the sound of a large metal door slamming shut in my mind, and God saying to me, "Oh, yes, you will."

When I returned home from my walk, I immediately contacted the local public school district to find out how to enroll Ty as a K-5 student for the coming school year. By ten o'clock that morning, I had met with the appropriate school official who completed Ty's enrollment in a matter of minutes. The sense of relief was overwhelming. The monkey was off my back, and I could finally rest. I continued to tell myself how ridiculous I had been to consider something like homeschooling.

From March until May of 1984 my life was incredibly peaceful—until all the parents of K-5 students in our neighborhood received a packet of information in the mail from the public school informing them of an orientation session for new parents and children. When I called the principal to ascertain why I had not received a packet, he very curtly informed me that I could not put my six-year-old in his K-5 program; Ty would enter school in the first grade. I knew if I calmly explained to him that his staff had guaranteed Ty a place in kindergarten, he would gracefully acquiesce. This principal let me know in no uncertain terms that his mind was made up.

I was still not extremely concerned because I had several acquaintances in the district office and knew them to be reasonable people. When I called and explained my predicament to district personnel, I could tell I may have reached an impasse. I used what I considered my trump card when I threatened to homeschool Ty if I would not be allowed to hold him back (as the school had already agreed to do). It was a bluff; but I knew no school administrator in South Carolina would encourage homeschooling if he could help it. To my amazement and horror, the man with whom I was speaking informed me that the school board had become lenient with that type of thing. What I came to find out later was they had approved one person to homeschool, and she had been a certified school teacher.

I had begun the homeschooling journey, albeit reluctantly and haltingly. But, as I examined and reflected upon the events of the past six months, I knew that God had closed all other doors and was indeed calling me to homeschool, beginning the adventure of our lives—including threats of jail and years spent in court and in the legislature.

People begin homeschooling for a variety of reasons. All homeschooling parents continue for one reason: it works! Great diversity exists among the types of people that homeschool. Because of the principles involved, homeschooling works for the doctor, the lawyer, the teacher, the pastor, the college professor, the bricklayer, and the truckdriver. Homeschooling works regardless of the parents' ethnic and/or socioeconomic backgrounds. Homeschooling works for Ph.D.'s and high school graduates. Homeschooling works for people of faith and people of no faith. Our message is simple: homeschooling works, and it can work for you!

Every person is different, and every family unique; but, in the following pages I will offer you some of the most convincing reasons parents choose to homeschool their children.

Passing the Baton

Faith in God is the most precious gift we can give our children. Homeschooling enables parents to grab hold of their faith and pass it on to the next generation. Scripture abounds with admonitions to parents to carefully raise and train their children to love the Lord. Let's begin in the Old Testament. The verses in Deuteronomy

6:4–7 are a powerful foundation for those families raising
their children in the Judeo-Christian ethic:

> Hear, O Israel! The Lord is our God, the Lord is
> one! And you shall love the Lord your God with all
> your heart and with all your soul and with all your
> might. And these words, which I am commanding
> you today, shall be on your heart; And you shall
> teach them diligently to your sons and shall talk of
> them when you sit in your house and when you
> walk by the way and when you lie down and when
> you rise up.

The Lord commands us to love Him with all of our
hearts, our souls, and our might. We are to teach our
children to do the same. Moses knew that an hour or two
on Sunday morning would not fill the bill—that to teach
children anything of a lasting nature requires time. Teaching our children is time-consuming and life-encompass-
ing. Homeschooling can be a tool for implementing the
Deuteronomic command; implicit in the command is that
you are your child's constant companion.

In the New Testament, Matthew 28:18–20 gives us
the Great Commission:

> And Jesus came up and spoke to them, saying, "All
> authority has been given to Me in heaven and on
> earth. Go therefore and make disciples of all the
> nations, baptizing them in the name of the Father
> and the Son and the Holy Spirit, teaching them to
> observe all that I commanded you; and lo, I am
> with you always, even to the end of the age."

The Greek verb for *go* in verse 29 can be translated,
"As *you are going*, make disciples . . ." The correlation between this and the Deuteronomic command is unmistak-
able. As we parents are going into the world, we are to
make disciples. Our first order of business should be to
make disciples of our children. A paraphrase of "As you
are going" could easily be, "As you sit in your house and

when you walk by the way and when you lie down and when you rise up."

Teaching our children to mightily love God is a unifying strand throughout Scripture. We have looked at passages in Deuteronomy and Matthew. The Proverbs are also filled with advice on raising children, as is the New Testament. In Ephesians 6:4, Paul admonishes fathers, "Do not provoke your children to anger; but bring them up in the discipline and instruction of the Lord." Homeschooling provides parents with the time they need to devote to the task of training the next generation.

Homeschooling—An American Tradition

When you decide to homeschool, you can rest assured that you are in good company. Just as the strands of parental responsibility in education are woven throughout the Bible, American history abounds with families who undertook the task of teaching their own. Homeschooling has been well represented in American history. John Wesley Taylor, Ph.D. and professor of education, tells us this:

> The home is mankind's first and most basic school. Home-centered education is as old as civilization itself, commencing long before state schools were organized or even conceived. Throughout much of American history, the primary center of instruction was the family. Parents were frequently the sole instructors of their offspring.[2]

Historian Steven Mintz and anthropologist Susan Kellogg concur:

> Three centuries ago the American family was the fundamental economic, educational, political, social, and religious unit of society. The family, not the isolated individual, was the unit of which church and state were made. The household was not only the focus of production, it was also the institution primarily responsible for the education of children,

the transfer of craft skills, and the care of the elderly and the infirm.[3]

In fact, homeschooling was the norm until the advent
of government schools in the midnineteenth century.

> Home instruction dominated the educational con-
> figuration of colonial America and continued to a
> lesser extent throughout the nineteenth century.
> After virtually disappearing at the turn of the cen-
> tury in the face of nearly universal institutional
> education at the elementary level, homeschooling
> has again become visible on our educational land-
> scape.[4]

What accounts for the robust reemergence of
homeschooling as an educational force during the last
two decades? Samuel Peavey, Ed.D., explained the situation this way when testifying before the Iowa State Board
of Education on home education:

> The renaissance of family-centered schooling is the
> natural outcome of a number of forces converging
> in a fateful era. Not the least of all these forces is
> the well-documented fact that both the American
> home and the American school have reached the
> lowest level of mediocrity in our history. The home-
> school is a pointed effort to salvage and safeguard
> values that once under girded schools as well as
> homes. Home education is a rejection of the trend
> toward almost total institutionalization of child rear-
> ing. It is a reaction to a decline in scholarship and
> character in the classroom. It is a testimony of faith
> in the family—a faith that is almost lost.[5]

Hundreds of thousands of families nationwide are em-
barking upon the homeschooling journey, with remarkable success. Families all across America are reclaiming
the heritage that was given us by our forefathers, the
heritage of directing the education of our children by
teaching them at home.

The Effectiveness of Tutorial Instruction

Homeschooling employs a tutorial method of instruction that is extremely efficient. In effect, each student has an Individual Educational Plan (IEP). Currently, IEPs in the classroom are only developed and implemented for special needs students because of the time and expense involved.

Students learning at home under the tutelage of a parent can progress at their own pace, regardless of ability. In this regard, homeschooling is the Rolls Royce of education. We buy cars made on an assembly line because most of us cannot afford the custom-built Rolls Royce. Our clothes would fit much better if we could have all of them tailor-made, but most of us visit department stores or discount stores to stay within our clothing budget. Boasting a height of five feet and no inches, I can not tell you the trials of finding clothing to fit without ridiculous amounts of alteration. In high school, I became so aggravated with shopping that I went on strike. My mother shopped and brought clothes home for me try on. If they fit, I kept them. If she had not been willing to shop for me, I would have worn the same outfit to school until it wore out. The process of finding clothes to fit had become totally laborious. Since I have become an adult, petite stores have made their debut. I no longer dread finding clothes because I know someone has designed clothes with my short arms, legs, and torso length in mind. The clothes have been *customized* for me—they fit.

Homeschooling to many children equates to my joy in finding the petite shop. Some have been in school, but the curriculum didn't fit. After a while, the process of learning becomes so burdensome the child quits trying. Like shopping for me, learning becomes too frustrating. When a child is home, the concerned parent can tailor a curriculum to fit his learning style or his abilities. A classroom teacher simply cannot individualize instruction for twenty to thirty students. There is just not enough time in the school day.

In 1990, I attended the National Board for Professional Teachers Standards Forum for North and South Carolina. I listened with amazement at the discussion circling around the hottest new educational "discovery"— all children can learn! Teachers must find out how to teach to each student. "All children can learn" is one of the foundational premises upon which homeschooling is built. The implementation of this premise occurs naturally and inexpensively (relatively speaking) in the home environment. Were you not your child's first teacher? You were there when he learned to walk and to talk. You know where he struggles, what motivates him, what frustrates him. You have built a personalized permanent record on him that is worth its weight in gold when it comes to knowing how to teach him effectively and efficiently.

Learning styles—how a child processes information— become pivotal in the homeschool. In the classroom they are a nuisance that hinder uniformity and order.

Attention to Readiness

Homeschooling not only allows you to determine *how* to teach your child, but also *when* to teach him. Readiness is an important concept in education, particularly in the elementary school years. Some children are ready for formal academics at age six; others are not ready until much later. In mass education, generalizations must be made. For instance, the compulsory attendance age in most states falls between five and seven years. Six-year-olds are placed in first grade and taught to read. Some children are bored stiff because they have been reading for years. Others are totally frustrated because they are physically incapable of reading at six years of age. In the home setting the parent can focus on each child's readiness and abilities, bypassing the boredom and frustration many children experience in school. Being able to give adequate attention to readiness is a major advantage of home education.

Control over Curriculum

In addition to determining how and when to teach your child, the homeschooling parent also controls *what* to teach. You are free to choose curriculum that reinforces the values that you and your family espouse. You can pray and read the Bible without violating Supreme Court edicts! You are free to teach creationism. You can teach American history and speak freely of the faith of the Puritans and Pilgrims. You are free to teach abstinence in sex education. You can teach Algebra I in sixth grade or tenth grade. You are able to teach from your own theological, moral, and/or philosophical basis. You have the ability to determine when and if it is appropriate to teach particular subjects.

Strengthening the Family Unit

Building family unity and maintaining the integrity of the family is a worthy motivation for homeschooling. Twentieth-century Americans have lost the value that was once placed on intimacy in the home. We put our six-week-old babies into daycare centers. Our children go from elementary school to after-school programs. Is it any wonder that by the time they are teen-agers they are disenfranchised from the adult world? We put our elderly parents in nursing homes. The home has ceased to be the center for care-giving as we have relegated our responsibilities to nurture to various institutions and to the state.

> And we should not give them a world that divides us into easy-to-market compartments, putting teen-agers here, grownups there, old folks in the attic. Because the most formative, most profound, and most lasting things in life, we will, without fail, learn not from books or videos or computers or classes, but from each other. In other words, it takes people to teach people.[6]

Homeschooling enables us to strengthen the family unit by restoring its dignity. The home once again becomes a place of industry and learning, of nurturing and caring, and of service and giving.

The Power of Companionship and Intimacy

Through homeschooling, we reclaim the family and build intimate relationships with our children that will bear fruit into eternity. Christ exemplifies the need for intimacy in the teacher-student relationship. Christ understood that to teach His disciples effectively, he must be with them. Even His name, Immanuel, means "God with us." As elementary as this sounds, do we really understand the importance of being with our children? The world tells us, "It's not the quantity of time you spend with your children that makes the difference; it's the quality of time." But, Christ was with His disciples when they were eating and sleeping and traveling and fussing and learning. He didn't differentiate between quality time and quantity time. He knew that to share the ecstasy of moments fraught with significance, He must also share the mundane, time-consuming tasks of life.

Christ taught through example, through parable, through hands-on experience, and through lecture. Although he made "guest appearances" to the multitudes, He limited His classroom to twelve. He gave His time and His heart to His disciples. The greatest opportunity for disciple-making parents will ever have on this earth is with their children. Christ gave the disciples intimacy and identity, two ingredients that are sorely missing in many of today's children and young people. Identity flows from the intimacy and unity found in strong families.

According to Jay Kesler, president of Taylor University, "The identity crisis of today's young people, individually and corporately, is the largest single factor affecting this generation. . . . [In the colonial era] identity came more from being linked to a family than from being just an individual. A young man was 'the Jones boy,' and he knew where he belonged and what he was to be."[7]

The Gift of Time

From the outside looking in, some parents are overwhelmed with the quantity of time homeschooling requires them to spend with their children. Oftentimes people react to homeschooling with disbelief: "I could never spend that much time with my kids; I can't wait for summer to end and school to begin." The abundance of time homeschooling provides a parent to interact with his child is one of the chief assets of homeschooling, even though in the beginning, many view it as a liability.

My husband and I began homeschooling because we were backed into a corner. Little did I know the abundant life waiting around the corner. The gift of time God gave me with my sons during the first year of homeschooling was precious. A deciding factor in our decision to continue homeschooling was the chunk of time school takes children from the home. School takes their prime time. When they come home, they are tired. They rest, and it's time to hit the books again. Are we being selfish by safeguarding the time we have with our children? John Taylor Gatto, New York State Teacher of the Year, reminds us in the foreword of *Government Nannies* that "kindergarten was created to be, and was quietly celebrated as, a gentle way to break the monopoly influence of mothers on their own children."[8]

The pace of life in our culture can be frantic. We often do not take the time we need to devote to one another—so many other things are vying for our time and attention. Homeschooling gives us the precious gift of time with our children: time to teach, as well as to model our faith; time to pursue excellence in academics; time to develop intimate relationships with our children; time to travel together; time to work and to serve together; and time to experience the richness, the abundance of life.

Hidden Treasures

My sons laugh at my scatterbrain ways. We are always looking for my keys, my purse, my contacts, my shoes. One particularly stressful morning we rose unusually early in order to finish most of our schoolwork before attending a hearing at the State House for which I bore great responsibility. I did not leave myself adequate time to dress, so I was frantic when I could not find my suit blouse or my shoes. My fourteen-year-old was scouring my closet when he amazed me with an astute observation that I did not appreciate at the time. "I didn't find your shoes or your blouse, but I did find my watch that has been missing for months. It seems like when you start searching for one thing, you find something even better."

Homeschooling is like that. We begin for one reason and are delightfully surprised at the other benefits we find along the way. I was terrified of the "socialization" issue when I began homeschooling. Now my husband and I both agree that if we had only one reason to choose homeschooling it would be socialization.

The Affirmation of Masculinity

Another hidden treasure for me as the mother of boys has been the opportunity to affirm their masculinity. When I was having Ty tested at age six by an eminently qualified Ph.D., she recommended that Ty be placed on Ritalin and in her report actually called him a "motor-mouth." I had Ty tested a second time by a male Ph.D. I'll never forget his assessment of Ty: "Zan, his vocabulary is incredible for a six-year-old boy. He is vivacious, energetic, and has wonderfully creative ideas. He is really a man's man, at age six."

That is when it dawned on me: every female teacher would probably view Ty as the female psychologist had, while male teachers would be able to appreciate his strengths. To most classroom teachers, probably all of them being female in the elementary level, Ty's effervescence, energy, and love of conversing would be a nuisance, not a delight. Asking Ty to sit at a desk quietly, six hours a day, would extinguish that internal spark he has always possessed. It would be like a prison. And to cope, he would surely have needed to be drugged.

Weldon Hardenbrook, author of *Missing from Action: Vanishing Manhood in America*, and whose wife has taught in public schools, also points out:

> The increasing absence of male influence from the home and the school has made it more difficult for each succeeding generation of young males to be secure in their masculinity. . . . As much as we might want to resist it, the truth is that one of the most sacred cows of our culture, the American public school, has had tremendously negative effects on the masculinity of the males of our society. Only father-absence exerts a greater feminizing influence on our boys than do the schools of our land.[9]

I am so thankful for the strong masculine role models my sons have had in their dad and both of their grandfathers. Homeschooling has been a vehicle that has allowed them extended time with these positive male counterparts.

The majority of children with learning disabilities are boys. Most troublemakers in the school setting are boys. Why do girls seem to enjoy school more and experience fewer problems than boys? Hardenbrook says when boys begin school "they are ready to learn things that contribute to the formation of their masculinity, but they are not ready for the restrictions that come upon them from a feminine atmosphere."[10]

History is replete with male figures who were simply not cut out for the classroom. Among the more obvious are Patrick Henry, Thomas Edison, and Albert Einstein. In his autobiography, the world-renowned photographer Ansel Adams had this to say about his boyhood years:

> I often wonder at the strength and courage my father had in taking me out of the traditional school

situation and providing me with extraordinary learning experiences. I am certain he established the positive direction of my life that otherwise, given my native hyperactivity, could have been confused and catastrophic. I trace who I am and the direction of my development to those years of growing up in our house . . . propelled especially by an internal spark tenderly kept alive and glowing by my father.[11]

Becoming Students of Our Children

One of the greatest joys of homeschooling is having the time to discover and develop the areas of strength and interest that each of our children possesses. Chuck Swindoll calls this understanding the *bent* of our children.[12] Dr. Raymond S. Moore has said that each child has an area of genius.[13] And, our assignment as parents is to find these areas and encourage our children in them. We must fan the flames of their enthusiasms and become our children's greatest cheerleaders.

Maximizing Strengths

In our adult lives we learn to maximize our strengths and compensate for, or at least minimize, our weaknesses. School is one of the few institutions in life where we are called upon to major on our weaknesses. Walter Barbe, Ph.D., makes this observation:

> As an adult, you have most likely learned through experience to transfer information from one channel to another, and to apply your learning strength in areas that are difficult. One of the sure signs of being an adult is knowing just what you are weak in. No one will ever catch us doing something willingly, especially in front of others, that we know we don't do well.
>
> Our children are not so lucky. In many academic settings, they are tested and confronted with their failures. They are given endless hours of practice,

not in their areas of strength, but in their areas of weakness. Eventually this can destroy their self-confidence and their willingness to learn.[14]

Am I saying it is not necessary to discipline a child to sit quietly or cope with situations that are difficult? Certainly not! However, we do need to individually assess each one of our children in order to know how he best learns.

The emphasis for both teachers and parents must be on the learning process, not just how much is learned. . . . Pressures to begin learning have contributed significantly to preschool enrollments. But the wisdom of such pressure is certainly debatable. We cannot teach our children all that they will need to know. The crux of the matter is not how early to start learning to learn more, but simply how to learn, how to enjoy learning so that the world is open to our children.[15]

Homeschooling allows us the freedom to focus on our child's strengths and interests. We can maximize his strengths without majoring on his weaknesses. We can help him to work through and compensate for his weaknesses without discouraging him in the process.

Turning Negatives into Positives

When parents are trying to decide whether to homeschool, I always encourage them to look at the inherent advantages of homeschooling, rather than dwelling on the disadvantages or problems in the school their children would attend or are attending. In the last two to three years, we are seeing what I consider a troubling trend: families leaving the public school system in droves. Parents are distraught over violence in schools, plummeting academic standards, the implementation of Outcome Based Education, and the escalation of federal intrusion into a school system that was once totally controlled at the state and/or local level.

The following letter expresses the sentiment and ambivalence that many parents are experiencing:

Dear SCAIHS Staff,

I would like to let you know how much support I felt from one of your employees even before I had applied for your service. . . . If my daughter's application is accepted I will finish her school year with "Home Teaching" and next school year I would teach not only my daughter but also add my son to this wonderful program.

I have always been a very involved parent at school, room mother, served on the PTA Board, and much more. I have also been an employee for the county schools. But it seems that the problems in our schools are getting much worse. The things that I have gone through with my daughter's school is more than any parent should go through for the full twelve years a student is in public school. I have no more faith in our school system. I am tired of being lied to, pacified, and am tired of everyone passing the buck. It is now time that I take over. I know that my children will learn, be safe, and be in a much better atmosphere. *I loved school and always wanted my children involved in school, but times have changed and at the present time I don't see them getting any better.* (emphasis mine)

I will be looking forward to hearing from you. Again, thank you for your listening ear and your support.[16]

As I dropped my daughter off at a gymnastics lesson last week, a friend asked if she could have a word with me. She is an outstanding public school teacher, and her children have been involved in the public school system all of their academic lives. Through tears, she asked me about homeschooling for her daughter. Midsentence she stopped herself and lamented that she, a public school stalwart, was having this conversation. Her daughter was falling through the cracks in her current school, and out of desperation she was seeking alternatives.

Many parents begin homeschooling because of a negative school situation. However, many of these same parents continue homeschooling because they discover many hidden treasures that are not apparent from the outside looking in.

Conclusion

We want our children to have an abundant, rich life. We want to dismantle the idea that education is limited to a classroom and textbooks and only occurs from eight o'clock in the morning to three o'clock in the afternoon, September through May. We want to communicate the concept that learning is a lifelong process, not a contrived and confining one. Education is as limiting or as exhilarating as we choose to make it. When we begin to view the world as our classroom, learning becomes an exciting adventure where we meet face to face the grandeur and awe of God's creation.

Chapter Two

Is There Any Evidence
Homeschooling Works?

The remarkable revival of home education in recent years may someday be seen as one of the most significant educational developments of this century. . . . I am not a promoter of homeschooling per se. I am a promoter of free choice among educational alternatives. It is my professional judgment that home-based education is one of the most significant and successful alternatives available to parents today.

—Sam B. Peavey, Ed.D., from observations and perspectives on home education prepared for the Iowa State Board of Education 5 August 1989

It was March of 1987. Ty was eight and completing the second grade; and John was six and enrolled in first grade although he was certainly not ready for the accompanying academic tasks. Given what happened when I requested that Ty begin first grade a year late, I dared not ask the school district "permission" to hold John back a year, even in a homeschooling program.

This would not have been a problem necessarily, except John was expected, required, by the school district to take the year-end standardized achievement test in the public school he would normally have attended. At age fourteen, 6-feet tall, and 185 pounds, this would have been no problem. But, at age six, John was quiet, sensitive, and just a little shy. There was another problem—he couldn't read.

I was using a reputable first grade curriculum, but John was just not ready yet for the formalized reading instruction. He is academically gifted, with an IQ that would qualify him for membership in the Menses society, but at six he was not reading, and we had this test looming ahead of us. I called a good friend, Dr. Loreen Itterman, who was the chairman of the Department of Elementary Education at Columbia International University. At my request, she tested John to see if I were to blame for his inability to read. After she tested John, she assured me his only problem was I had been pushing him too much: If I would leave him alone, he would be fine.

I desperately wanted to leave him alone and let him develop at his own pace. But, I felt tremendous pressure for John to do well on the two tests he was required by law to take: the Comprehensive Test of Basic Skills, a nationally normed achievement test, and the Basic Skills Assessment Program, a state-developed assessment measure. If he did not do well, the school district could require me to discontinue my homeschooling program. Dr. Itterman, my attorney, and I all wrote letters to the school district requesting that John's first grade testing be postponed until the next year, to no avail.

The first week of testing came. I assured John it was nothing to worry about and told him how to take the test. "Mark *a* for the first question, count to five, and move on to number two." When he asked me why he was to count to five between each question, I reminded him that pausing between questions would keep others from noticing that he could not yet read. We laughed, and I assured him that I certainly was not worried about his not reading yet—because I knew he was such a smart boy—and God surely was not upset. Everybody John cared about was happy, so with no concern at all he marched into that school room with all the confidence in the world.

On the other hand, I went home and sobbed, knowing what the results would be on that test. I did not want to quit homeschooling John, but I knew that my school district would most certainly deny my request to homeschool John unless a miracle occurred. Then and there, on my knees, between sobs, I asked God for a miracle. I remember praying, "Lord, if you are in this thing called homeschooling, I need your help now more than ever." I reminded God of how he protected the Hebrew midwives from Pharaoh's punishment and had even blessed them because they refused to harm the male babies as they were born (Exod. 1:15–21). I prayed that, in the same way, God would protect John and me from retribution by the school district for low test scores. I asked God to blind their eyes to his scores.

The summer came, and with the summer came the test scores. I can remember trembling as I opened the letter from the district bearing John's scores. The scores were terrific! As a matter of fact, some of them were perfect scores. The district had sent me scores that belonged to another John Tyler, who happened to live in our same small neighborhood. He was older, bore a different middle initial, and had a different, though similar, address. God had answered my prayers, protected my child, preserved my ability to homeschool for the next year, and encouraged me in a way I have not forgotten to this day.

The next year things clicked for John. He again marched into the schoolroom confidently. When he finished, I asked him how things went. I'll never forget his classic response, "Mom, you can't believe how much easier it is to take a test when you can read what's on it!" His test scores were excellent that year, with most of them being in the upper nineties in terms of percentile ranking.

Standardized test results are the easiest way to objectively measure the academic effectiveness of homeschooling. As the above story demonstrates, there are problems connected with standardized testing. These problems are causing even the educational community to rely on their use less heavily than they have in the past. Standardized testing does not do a good job of measuring critical thinking skills or the ability to communicate verbally or the ability to write (compose). Standardized tests are supposed to be used as diagnostic tools, not as meters to determine the worth of the student or the teacher. Some children don't test well, even if they have been taught well and have learned well.

However, standardized testing does have some merit in the educational scheme of things. These nationally normed tests do provide an unbiased measure in some academic areas. We need to strive to present educators, legislators, and the community around us with unbiased evidence that homeschooling works. Even though many people do not understand homeschooling, they understand test scores. When they see the composite test scores of homeschoolers, they may not become fans, but they see that homeschooling works and become a little less hostile or skeptical.

All SCAIHS members between grades three and twelve must participate in standardized testing. Is it because we on the staff just love standardized testing? Absolutely not. We follow the state testing laws for public school students as closely as we can because it is important to legislators and other public officials. As you will see in the following paragraphs, homeschoolers do very well on standardized testing because homeschooling works. I use the SCAIHS test scores on an annual basis with legislators and other groups as a public relations tool. As long as students are doing well, even opponents have little reason to challenge us.

Statistics from the most extensive sampling of home school achievement to date once again support the fact that homeschooling works, and works well. This study, conducted by the Home School Legal Defense Association (see appendix C), involved over sixteen thousand students in grades kindergarten through twelve from all fifty states. These students took the Iowa Test of Basic Skills during the spring of 1994. Dr. Brian Ray, president of the National Home Education Research Institute (se:

appendix D), analyzed the test results provided by the Riverside Publishing Company. With nationally normed tests like the Iowa, percentile ranking is used to indicate the percentage of students who have achieved above and below a particular score. The national average is the 50th percentile, while the average range begins at the 24th percentile and extends to the 76th percentile.[1]

According to this study, 79 percent of homeschooled students scored above the national average, compared to 50 percent of the conventional school population. The national average for homeschooled students in reading was at the 79th percentile, while the national average for homeschooled students in language was at the 73d percentile. Math scores for homeschooled students averaged at the 73d percentile also. (Remember, average is the 50th percentile.) Perhaps one of the most significant discoveries of this study is that over 54 percent of the homeschooled students scored in the top quartile of achievement. That is more than double the national average of 25 percent. Seventy-nine percent of the homeschooled students scored above the 50th percentile, compared to only 50 percent of the total school-aged population. These results are phenomenal![2]

Test scores of members of the South Carolina Association of Independent Home Schools from 1991 through 1994 are very similar to the national statistics on homeschooled students. SCAIHS students were required to take the Stanford 8 Achievement Test, the same nationally norm-referenced test required of public school students, during the same time period. According to the South Carolina State Department of Education, the primary indicator of achievement on nationally normed standardized achievement tests is the percentage of students scoring above the 50th national percentile. *The South Carolina Norm-Referenced Testing Program 1991 Report* states, "Performance in a subject is considered weak if considerably more students score 'below average' and fewer students score 'above average' than the norm group. Performance is considered strong if the opposite conditions hold. In the norm group, 23 percent of the norm group scored 'below average,' 54 percent average, and 23 percent 'above average.' "[3] An overall analysis of the test results, both nationally and statewide, indicate that the academic performance of homeschooled students is very strong.

- In 1991, 76 percent of SCAIHS students scored above the 50th percentile;
- In 1992, 74 percent of SCAIHS students scored above the 50th percentile;
- In 1993, 77 percent of SCAIHS students scored above the 50th percentile; and
- In 1994, 72 percent of SCAIHS students scored above the 50th percentile.

SCAIHS was conceived amidst legal and legislative controversy. We spent much of our first two years in court. By the end of 1991, the State Department of Education, under the direction of a newly elected superintendent, was ready, as were we, to put an end to the seemingly endless rounds of litigation. All parties involved reached a consensus that legislation establishing the authority of SCAIHS to approve and supervise homeschooling programs in South Carolina would end the pending lawsuits and provide a satisfactory answer to the "homeschooling problem" in our state. Both Houses of the General Assembly had to approve the SCAIHS bill. The bill generated great debate at the Senate Education Committee meeting. The debate all but ended as a spokesperson for the State Department of Education addressed the committee. She presented the composite of the SCAIHS test scores and reminded the legislators that they were deregulating schools with test scores less significant than ours. The academic achievement of the homeschooled students was so strong that it positively impacted our legislation, enabling it to pass.

State Departments of Education in several states have conducted their own studies to ascertain the academic achievement of homeschooled students. In Alaska, Oregon, and Tennessee, homeschooled students have scored well above average on standardized achievement tests. Results in the states of Washington and Montana also demonstrate that homeschooled students are scoring consistently above average on standardized achievement tests.[4]

Why Does Homeschooling Work?

In the chapter "Why Would I Want to Homeschool?" we discussed several of the advantages of homeschooling. These advantages produce positive educational results: the tutorial advantage, the educational efficiency, the constant interaction with adults, the attention to readiness. Other factors contribute heavily to the success of homeschools as well.

The Power of the Family Unit in Society

The family is the basic unit of any civilization. Strong families yield a powerful society. Conversely, if the foundation of any structure is weak, it will eventually crumble. In the twentieth century, we have done everything we can to undermine and weaken the family. Parents have willingly abdicated responsibilities that are God-given, and the government has been eager to step in and take over. The end result has been a total disaster. We have all but handed our children over to be raised and nurtured by the state. Schools continue to lengthen their days and their school years, and lower the compulsory attendance age; many now provide a wide array of social services in addition to academic training. We have become so accustomed to the government providing services that have historically fallen in the family's domain, that we don't even stop to question the wisdom of the arrangement. God never intended for institutions to nurture children. He created the family for that purpose.

The family is the basic institution in society. God instituted the family to be foundational to all other institutions. The family is every child's first teacher. Theologian R.J. Rushdoony says, "The family is man's first state,

church, and school. It is the institution which provides
the basic structure of his existence and most governs his
activities."[5] The family is a "framework which extensively
and profoundly shapes his concept of himself and of life
in general."[6]

The family is a defining institution for every individual in society. Homeschooling enables families to give
"positive definitions" to children by working together,
studying together, serving together, worshiping together,
and playing together.

The benefits of homeschooling are not limited to af-
fluent, well-educated families. We have had many families
in SCAIHS who live, or have lived, below the poverty
level. These families could qualify for free or reduced
lunch programs, along with a whole host of programs
offered through the school systems. Instead, they have
chosen to homeschool their children. Lack of income does
not interfere with a parent's ability to love, nurture, and
teach her children. The poor person is as capable of
loving her children and providing a stable home environment as is the rich parent.

One mother who contacted our office lives on a very
limited income. Although she is a high school graduate,
she does not present herself as a well-educated person. I
wondered how she could cope with the financial and academic pressures of homeschooling without short-chang-
ing her children. She has dealt with the educational pressure by purchasing a structured curriculum with in-depth
teachers' aids and by joining SCAIHS to provide her with
the one-on-one counseling—curriculum and otherwise—
she has needed. Of the financial pressure, all I can say is,
Where there is a will, there is a way. This mother is
successfully teaching her children, making ends meet,
and educating herself as well.

As society has deteriorated in the last half of the twentieth century, we are forced to evaluate the way we have
abdicated the power and function of the home to various
institutions. Even good institutions are no match for the

real thing—the family. Now even secular educators and politicians are being forced to acknowledge what God has known for eternity: a strong family life is crucial to the spiritual, moral, emotional, and intellectual development of the child, regardless of where the child is formally educated. The family has been instituted by God and charged by God to teach and to train. What God ordains, He will bless.

The Power of Strong Families and Parental Involvement

Nick Stinnett, Ph.D., conducted several nationwide studies to identify characteristics of strong families. After analyzing the data collected from studying three thousand families, Dr. Stinnett concluded that strong families "are committed to the family; spend time together; have good family communication; express appreciation to each other; have a spiritual commitment; and are able to solve problems in a crisis."[7]

This reads like a prescription for homeschooling. Many strong families homeschool. Many who begin homeschooling become stronger and stronger as family units. Even families that are tentative about homeschooling discover that as they learn to work together (and it does take effort on everyone's part), they become stronger than they ever imagined possible. It is like any type of physical exercise. The first few weeks can be painful at times as you exercise muscles you haven't used in years. But, the longer you work at it, the easier and more exhilarating it becomes.

Notice number six in Dr. Stinnett's list: Strong families are able to solve problems in a crisis. Homeschooling families are not immune to problems or crises. But, the effective homeschooling family learns to work through them together.

In his speech entitled "Strong Families, Strong Schools," Dick Riley, the United States secretary of education, made an impassioned plea for the American public to pay closer attention to the role of parents as children's most important teachers. In a strong endorsement of the importance of the family in education, Riley declared, "The American family is the rock on which a solid education can and must be built."[8]

Riley suggested a sevenfold plan to help parents implement practices to strengthen the family unit:

1. Prioritize your time to make learning together as a family a reality.
2. Set high standards and expectations for you and your children.
3. Limit television viewing on school nights.
4. Read together.
5. Encourage your children to take the "tough" classes and get involved in their homework.
6. Insist on daily school attendance.
7. Communicate openly with your children about the values you want them to have.[9]

Homeschooling is the epitome of parental involvement. The homeschooling parents I come into contact with would view Riley's seven steps as a bare minimum— a starting point—for involvement in the lives of their children. To read Riley's speech with the emphasis on parental involvement was refreshing; however, it is discouraging to note that many of the professional educators who are touting the "new banner" of parental involvement are very much opposed to homeschooling. As the kids say, go figure!

The question has been asked, Is homeschooling an academically superior educational method compared to conventional schooling? John Wartes is a public high school counselor as well as a homeschooling researcher and father. In response to this question, he cites the problems associated with conducting the proper research to answer the question. A study would have to be designed to show that any difference in academic achievement is not due to other factors. "For example, it is commonly acknowledged that the homeschoolers have *parents who are more dedicated and supportive than usual* [emphasis mine].

Is the academic outcome a result of the homeschooling or of having supportive parents?"[10]

In answering his question, I would say the two elements—homeschooling and dedicated, supportive parents—are inextricably bound. Parental involvement and dedication are the heart of homeschooling; take out the heart, and it dies. Homeschooling is the epitome of parental involvement. Without parental support there can be no homeschooling.

Thousands of homeschooling families testify daily to the power of parental involvement in education. Homeschools are producing well-educated, well-adjusted students at a fraction of the cost of traditional education. Many times parents have less formal training and education than their professional counterparts. How can these families consistently produce children of this caliber without the resources public schools have at their disposal? The power of parental involvement and a strong family life are powerful conduits for an effective, efficient learning environment.

The Power of Parents as Teachers

Part of the answer to the above question, How can homeschooling families produce well-educated, well-adjusted students without the resources that public schools have at their disposal? can be found in what makes an effective teacher. A large part of teacher-training in the university setting is geared to classroom management. I am not critical of this: it is the nature of classroom instruction. A teacher must learn to manage twenty to thirty students of different abilities, with different backgrounds, and different levels of parental expectations. It is a formidable task at best. Add to the equation the fact that many parents are apathetic, and the teacher's job becomes increasingly difficult. A tutorial style of teaching circumvents the needs for those types of skills. Concerned, loving parents already possess the key ingredients inherent in the art of good teaching.

In "The Art of Good Teaching," author and professor Jack H. Groomsman postulates that the goal of outstanding teachers and managers is to bring out the best in the people under their care. Respect for those for which they are responsible and a desire to see them succeed governs their behavior. He gives ten qualities that excellent teachers and managers share. I have included some of them below:

1. They "really listen" to their students or employees.
2. They are genuinely interested in those under their care.
3. They have clear expectations.
4. They are eager to teach their students what they know.
5. They encourage positive behavior and discourage "unacceptable performance."
6. They are flexible.
7. They exhibit enthusiasm and maintain a sense of humor.
8. They find positive ways to motivate their students and employees to live up to their full potential.[11]

Homeschooling parents have an ardent desire to bring out the best in the people for whom they are responsible. While each of us has areas to improve, we have a desire to see our children succeed and thrive more than anyone else on the face of this earth. This motivation, this desire, according to Groomsman, is the prerequisite for being an outstanding teacher.[12]

The Power of Motivation, Love, and Self-Sacrifice

The success of homeschooling is due in large part to parent-teachers who will do anything within their power to help their students learn and succeed. Motivation and love for our children enable us to overcome what to others would be insurmountable odds. I have seen parents learn Spanish, trigonometry, and physics for the sake of their children. I have watched mothers take night jobs to make ends meet, allowing them freedom during the day-time hours to teach their children. Parents have risked jail and legal actions to teach their children at home. (Thankfully, this doesn't happen frequently anymore.) This self-sacrifice, this willingness to do whatever it takes, is what causes homeschooling not only to work, but to flourish.

Christ Himself said, "Greater love has no one than this, that one lay down his life for his friends."[13] Christ poured three years of His life into His disciples. He ate with them, fished with them, traveled with them, taught them, rebuked them, and loved them. And, after pouring out His life for them, He died for them—and us. In Philippians 2:3–8, Paul tells us to follow Christ's example:

> Do nothing out of selfish ambition or vain conceit, but in humility consider others better than your-selves. Each of you should look not only to your own interests, but also to the interests of others. Your attitude should be the same as that of Christ Jesus: Who, being in very nature God, did not consider equality with God something to be grasped, but made Himself nothing, taking the very nature of a servant, being made in human likeness. And being found in appearance as a man, he humbled himself and became obedient to death—even death on a cross.

The Power of Parental Knowledge

Dr. Peavey says, "It has been most interesting to me to see homeschool parents with high school diplomas doing as well or better than my certified teachers as measured by their students' standardized test results. Those parents revealed some things to me about living, loving, and learning, that I was never taught by my dis-tinguished professors at Harvard and Columbia."[14]

As a society we have undermined, undervalued, and underestimated the importance and the power of the family—of parenthood and motherhood. The intimacy and affection found in healthy homes provide the ideal basis, environment, and catalyst for learning. Do not underestimate what you bring to your child as a teacher. You have been with him since the day he was born. You know what he struggles with, what he's good at. You understand his temperament; you know what motivates him and what discourages him. Parents are in unique positions to discover the genius in each child. Study your child. Find his area of genius—the gifts and talents he has to contribute to the world—and fan the flame.

When a classroom teacher sees your child in class for the first time, she may have read a permanent record and maybe conducted a thirty-minute parent-teacher conference. But, even by the end of the school year, she will not know a fraction of what you know about your own child. While assembly-line, mass-production education works for some, the Rolls Royce of education is still one-to-one instruction springing from an intimate, loving relationship.

In his book *Growing Wise in Family Life*, Charles Swindoll discusses the importance of carving time out of our busy schedules to become students of our children.

> Give your child the time it takes to find out how he or she is put together. Help your child know who he or she is. Help them know themselves so that they learn to love and accept themselves as they are. Then as they move into a society that seems committed to pounding them into another shape, they will remain true to themselves, secure in their independent walk with their God.

> I have begun to realize that secure, mature people are best described in fifteen words. They know who they are . . . they like who they are . . . they are who they are. They are *real*.[15]

All parents, regardless of where their children are educated, need to become students of their children.

Homeschoolers do not have a corner on the market. However, homeschooling does facilitate the process by providing the time, as well as a constant forum for interaction and discussion.

The Power of Experiential Learning

According to John Wesley Taylor, Ph.D.,

> Home-centered education is educationally sound. It is a viable educational alternative. The home is an ideal environment for fostering creativity, inquiry, and practical learning. The home school provides for flexibility of schedule and program. It permits individualized, innovative approaches to education. There is opportunity for frequent feedback and intimate warmth, for independent diversification and non-vicarious experience. The child is given a chance to explore and discover. He participates in active learning—the doing. He can experience learning—not just read or hear about it. He learns how to learn.[16]

Frequent feedback and intimate warmth, independent diversion and nonvicarious experience. What a rich life! Logistically, a classroom teacher cannot provide the feedback, the flexibility, the attention to learning styles, or the emphasis on exploration and experiential learning that the homeschool provides.

Experiential learning is a powerful educational tool. Homeschooling lends itself to experiential learning. With a little imagination and research on your part, you can tap into this advantage of homeschooling—the ability to facilitate and reinforce learning through nonvicarious experience.

Following are some of the things we have done as a family. I provide these simply as a way to get your creative juices flowing. Your interests, and those of your children, will be different from mine.

When the boys were in third and fifth grade, we did a unit study on Washington, D.C. Along with reading and research, each boy was required to build a model of a famous building or monument in the capital city. Upon completion, we used Joe's frequent flyer points to fly to Washington and spent a week sightseeing and visiting the historic sites we had studied. Another study we did that was particularly memorable was the history of flight. Ty built a model glider, a small motorized plane (with a lot of help from a friend), and read several books on flight. Then, as a family, we traveled to Ohio to visit a museum on the history of flight. We did one unit on space, which culminated with the boys spending a week at Space Camp in Florida. Studying that is reinforced by experience is very profitable and memorable.

The preceding unit studies were fun, in spite of involved preparations and "fund-raising." However, some of our most significant learning experiences as a family have been painful. In March of 1986, I lost a baby during the sixth month of pregnancy. During the traumatic birth and death of Joy, our daughter, my survival became questionable as well. In the wake of this ordeal, I found myself physically and emotionally exhausted. I also found myself wishing that the boys, then ages five and seven, were in school so that I could recover and deal with my grief in peace.

To make matters worse, while I was in the hospital, we were notified by the State Department of Education that the first public hearing ever to be held in South Carolina on homeschooling would be scheduled for May 12. (They were required to give me sixty days advanced notice.) Joe and I had no choice but to begin planning the hearing from my hospital room. Between tears and prayers, we made plans and contacted potential speakers and concerned parents. When I went home from the hospital, I wanted to crawl in a hole—and give myself time to recover physically and emotionally from the trauma of Joy's birth and death. Instead, we went home and continued teaching the boys and planning for the hearing. Our families and our church ministered to us in incredible ways through emotional support, meal preparation, and watching the boys. However, with much work to be done, it was not a time of idyllic rest and recovery.

In retrospect, Ty and John grew as much during that period as Joe and I did. Had they been in school, they would have missed out on a valuable lesson on the preciousness of life and the reality of death. Because they were homeschooled, the boys were intimately involved with preparations for the new baby. We discussed the coming of a new baby throughout the day, and the boys accompanied me to most of my doctor's appointments. Their anticipation of a new brother or sister was great, due in large part to their involvement in my daily life. The boys were present for the ultrasound where Joy's certain death at birth was announced, along with the incredible health risks I was facing. They had been planning for six months for a new baby; their expectations had been dashed no less significantly than had mine and Joe's. Their excitement and their grief were as genuine and heartfelt as ours. Grieving would have been much easier for me if I had been alone. However, God changed all of our lives through the birth and death of Joy and gave us as a family a heightened awareness of the reality of heaven and life eternal. This was more life-transforming than any academic course on death and dying, which has become part of many schools' curriculum.

When Elizabeth was born in September of 1987, there was great rejoicing in the Tyler family. After the trauma of losing Joy, Elizabeth's birth was especially sweet. A few weeks before Elizabeth's birth, Ty, age nine, asked, "How will I get this baby to love me?" I remember giving him an inadequate answer, as I continued on with whatever it was I was doing. Because of homeschooling, Ty and John have had the freedom to be intimately involved in Elizabeth's life from the very beginning. Because of the age difference, there has been no sibling rivalry. They have cherished her, loved her, taught her, enjoyed her, protected her—yes, and aggravated her. Watching two

strapping teen-age boys become so close to a younger
sister has been one of the deepest joys of my
homeschooling experience.

When Elizabeth was twelve weeks old, Ty reminded
me of the question he had posed before her birth. "Mom,
now I know how to make a baby love you. You take care
of her and love her and spend time with her, even when
you don't feel like it." Ty learned at nine what many men
fail to learn in a lifetime: children are both a joy and a
responsibility.

In June of 1994, Ty spent three weeks with a study
group overseas. At one point, the group with which Ty
was traveling was confronted with a situation that could
have been a little frightening; police asked them to leave
a college campus, giving them little more than a few
hours notice to gather their belongings and leave. When
we asked Ty if he had been scared, he looked at me
comically, and said, "No, mom, I'm used to this. Remember we've been homeschooling for ten years now!" Even
our legal difficulties have served as a training ground for
our children.

The lessons of life are learned as parents and children experience together the peaks and valleys of human
existence. Children learn as their parents involve them in
all aspects of life—learning, serving, working, playing,
and worshiping.

> The adult world might at times be confusing, un-
> pleasant, and even wrought with pain, but just as
> often it can be filled with laughter, or love, or
> concern and caring. And whatever else it will be, it
> will be rich in complexity and emotion, and will
> give children not only an understanding of their
> own species, but—just as important—a sense of
> inclusion in it.[17]

Perhaps the best hands-on training my children have
received has been in civics. They have personally witnessed all three branches of government at work—the

executive, the judicial, and the legislative. They have worked in political campaigns since they were eight and ten years old. They understand the power of grassroots efforts. They have followed bills from a concept to the implementation. Being civic-minded and politically involved is a natural part of their lives. We were at the check-out counter in the grocery store when Ty was ten. He overheard two adults ahead of us engaged in a lively discussion about an aggravating issue in the community. He said, "Excuse me for interrupting, but have you ever thought about changing the law?" The startled adults listened as Ty explained the recent homeschooling legislative effort.

Later that same year, Ty asked me if the tour guides in the State House were paid or volunteer positions. As I wondered what prompted that question, he continued, "I've spent so much time down here, I think I could conduct those tours, and make some money at the same time!" Ty is now working as a page in the South Carolina Senate. The Senate is a grand classroom for learning the lessons of citizenry and civics first-hand. Most adults are uninvolved in government because it is too intimidating or because they are apathetic. If our children are comfortable and familiar with the process of government, they have a greater chance of becoming involved, effective adults.

As we explore the concept of experiential learning, I do not mean to imply that all learning is "fun" or even "totally meaningful" in the homeschool environment. My children are required to do many things that they would rather not. But, due to the nature of homeschooling, opportunities do abound for creativity and nonvicarious experience.

The Power of Example and Service

Most homeschooling families can complete most of the academic portion of their day in the morning hours, leaving the afternoons free for special projects, community service, and other enriching activities. You can use this freedom to teach your children to become sacrificially involved in the lives of others. In an age that teaches self-fulfillment and hedonism, we must continually strive to provide service opportunities for our children, enabling them to learn the joy of giving and service first-hand.

Some opportunities occur naturally; some take work. When the boys were very young, I had to be creative in finding ways that they could serve others without being in the way! Most volunteer organizations do not want younger children around. During the first semester of each year, we focused on Christmas projects as opportunities for service. In September we would begin work on what we referred to as "widow baskets." The boys would memorize a long Scripture passage—twenty or so verses from the Christmas story, for instance—and learn all four verses to a couple of Christmas hymns. We would work on a special art project to include in the baskets, and, a month before Christmas, we would begin a special cooking project— like making jelly or hot fudge sauce or pies—things that could be stored or frozen and included in the baskets at Christmas. The last Christmas that we made and delivered our widow baskets, we took them to over twenty widows, church staff, relatives, and neighbors—a time-consuming project as the boys would recite their verses, sing their songs, and usually give detailed explanations of every item in the basket. We could make only two or so deliveries an evening. As the boys have gotten older, we have discontinued the baskets in lieu of other things; but what we gained as a family from those months of working on those little baskets is more precious than gold. We focused our attention on someone besides ourselves for months. We talked about Scripture passages that spoke specifically of widows. As we thought of the men and women in our congregation, we prayed for them more; and, as we visited them, we developed hearts that were more loving and compassionate. Sometimes our little widow baskets weren't much to look at. The significance came in channeling the ever-present energy of two little boys into the needs of other people.

Another thing we have done consistently over the years is to work with Project Angel Tree, a ministry to prison inmates and their children sponsored by Prison Fellowship. In the early years, we were stationed at an island in a mall for hours at a time. I still have visions of the boys passing out fliers, explaining why all little children need Christmas presents. The boys would also wrap the presents that many brought in for the children of inmates. The biggest challenge for me was figuring out how to rewrap all those presents without the boys catching me!

When my grandparents were in nursing homes, a very natural part of our lives was to visit them. The elderly love having little children around. If you have no grandparents living or close enough to visit, your church or any nursing home can help you find someone who would love to be loved.

Older children can work as candy stripers or volunteer in dozens of other capacities. Many cities have one organization that serves as an information source for most other volunteer organizations. Get involved in the lives of the handicapped. The Special Olympics can be a great place for the family to volunteer together. The ministry of Joni and Friends[18] can give assistance in locating institutions or individuals in your locale that are in need of volunteers.

Many families adopt special projects as a way to serve the community together. I have known families who have cleaned their churches or the homes of shut-ins. Others have delivered Meals-on-Wheels. The possibilities for ministry and service are endless. We live in a hurting world. Many government programs are begun because of the extreme needs around us and the lack of concern and actions on the part of the citizenry.

Short-term missions projects are an extremely effective way to expose your children to different cultures and

to missions at the same time. Some families travel together. Sometimes teens go with other homeschoolers,
youth groups, or missions organizations. In February,
thanks to the generosity of Gregg and Becky, my middle
son had a life-changing experience. Gregg is a periodontist
with a heart for missions. He and another dentist arranged a missions trip to an impoverished area of Mexico.
They took Gregg's thirteen-year-old son, David, and our
fourteen-year-old son, John, to be the "dental assistants."
John is taking Spanish II now; and, from a language
standpoint, the trip was an incredible opportunity. The
cultural exposure was phenomenal and life-changing, as
they witnessed a level of poverty they had never experienced. As more and more patients lined up outside the
door of the building in this Mexican town, the load became overwhelming as they had only a week to minister
to the needs of so many. In response, Gregg and the
other dentist taught David and John how to give injec-
tions, pull teeth, and take sutures. I was floored and
amazed. Gregg's willingness to take John to Mexico
changed his life. Not only did it give John a greater heart
for missions and the needs of others, it gave him career
direction as well. He is now set on pursuing a career in
some area of dentistry.

Do you love to cook, or to sew, or to organize? Are
you a nurse, doctor, computer guru, teacher, builder, or
an all-around hard worker? Use your natural abilities,
talents, and training as the basis for your volunteer work.
Then, you can really enjoy it. Get your children involved
as well. It takes longer, and the end result may not be as
pretty, but you will be participating in raising a generation of servants and workers fit for the kingdom of heaven.

Remember that homeschooling is a means to an end,
not an end in itself. Use the increased time you have as
a family to minister to the needs of others. You will find
yourself truly blessed as you remember it really is more
blessed to give than to receive.

The Power of Time

If homeschooling success had to be reduced to one word, I would choose *time*. Time is the fulcrum on which all else balances. In order to homeschool, parents must commit their time—perhaps the biggest sacrifice of all in our hurried, frenetic society. It takes time to choose curriculum and make lesson plans. It takes time to teach. It takes time to study and know your students. It takes time to read together. By investing this time in your children, you will inevitably sacrifice time in an area that you enjoy. But remember the old adage, "Children spell love t-i-m-e." As we take the time to work with our children, learn with our children, serve with our children, and interact with our children, we are equipping them for life in the real world, as well as speaking volumes to them about their worth and importance as human beings. The time we invest in our children while they are home will reap great benefits in the future and in eternity.

Paul's words in Galatians 6:7–9 are both sobering and encouraging: "Do not be deceived: God cannot be mocked. A man reaps what he sows. The one who sows to please his sinful nature, from that nature will reap destruction; the one who sows to please the Spirit, from the Spirit will reap eternal life. Let us not become weary in well-doing, for at the proper time we will reap a harvest if we do not give up."

The Power of Identity and Intimacy

In speaking of the hurried, frantic pace most parents must endure, Secretary of Education Riley made these comments, "I believe that we are missing something far deeper in all this rushing around. We are letting our children grow up, at times, almost alone—and disconnected."[19] Alone—and almost disconnected. This one insightful observation by Riley sums up why homeschooling works so well. Children, regardless of age, cannot flourish when they are alone and disconnected. They need committed adults in their lives who love them and cherish them and want to see them succeed. They need to know that even (especially) through the storms and trials of life our commitment to them does not waver.

Alienation seems to be the curse of the nineties. Spouses are alienated from one another. Parents and children are alienated. Teen-agers are alienated from everyone! We live in a fragmented society, with no moral code or absolute values. Many times our children, especially our teen-agers, seem to be wandering in a vacuum—separated from everything meaningful in life. Homeschooling provides us with a vehicle to establish family unity and identity. As homeschooling families work together, a sense of identity is established. As we as parents study our children and learn their strengths and weaknesses, we can help them develop a sense of purpose and destiny as they equip themselves to take their God-ordained position in this world.

A Word about Educational Trends

Homeschooling parents are often intimidated by the world of the professional educator. We wonder whether we really are equipped to handle the challenges of teaching like the one who has been certified. Most teaching courses teach educators how to manage a class. Teaching twenty to forty children (who are strangers at the beginning of the school year) is quite different than teaching one or two or even seven or eight of your own.

The ever-changing trends in education should tip us off that professional educators are constantly looking for more effective teaching theories, and public education is in a constant state of flux. No teacher at home or at school ever "arrives." Do you know what one of the hottest new developments in educational reform is? Parental involvement![20] The eighth goal in the Goals 2000 standards is parental involvement. Educators everywhere are calling for more parental involvement. This is one trend in education we do not need to be intimidated by.

Mentoring and *shadowing* have become buzzwords lately among educators. Both of these connote the idea of matching students with competent adults, usually in a specific field of interest, expertise, or vocation. The concept is an excellent one; I'm glad society is waking up and realizing just how much students, even older high school students, need adult role models. Mentoring and shadowing occur very naturally in the homeschool environment; in many ways, these concepts form the basis of homeschooling.

Another hot topic in education today is the concept of "MegaSkills." In the *NEA Today*, NEA President Keith Geiger urges his readers to recognize the "all-important reality" that when it comes to equipping children with the "attitudes and behaviors" that lead to success in school, there is no place like home: "Home is where children can best develop the attributes so crucial to learning—confidence, motivation, effort, responsibility, initiative, perseverance, caring, teamwork, common sense, and problem solving."[21]

Dorothy Rich, veteran educator, has coined a word for these attributes: MegaSkills—the inner engines of learning.[22] MegaSkills workshops are being offered around the country to teach parents how to inculcate these traits in their children. Did you know you have been teaching MegaSkills everyday of your homeschooling life?

I am amazed at how many of these ideas are concepts that homeschooling parents have been incorporating into their schools for decades, at no cost to the state or taxpayers! Take heart in your homeschooling; have confidence. You are on the cutting edge of education. I also find it encouraging, if not somewhat amusing, that educators, many of them totally secular in their orientation, are spending thousands of dollars to research and implement ideas that we have known all along. God does have a sense of humor! You can rest easy knowing you're not being left behind when it comes to educational trends. We're up to snuff on parental involvement, mentoring and shadowing, and MegaSkills.

Conclusion

Does homeschooling work? Academically, homeschooled children are doing well; statistics speak for themselves. Beyond that, homeschooling is providing a vehicle to help parents reclaim their families. Homeschooling allows us to give the time to our children that they so desperately need, to give our children a sense of identity and purpose, to give them a sense of destiny, and to teach them to walk humbly with our God.

Chapter Three

Is Homeschooling Legal?

The child is not a mere creature of the state; those who nurture and direct his destiny have the right, coupled with the high duty, to recognize and prepare him for additional obligations.

—The Supreme Court of the United States

Homeschooling Is Legal in All Fifty States

My heart for being politically involved in homeschooling issues and helping mothers prepare themselves legally grows from my own experiences when we began homeschooling. Let me remove all doubt at the onset: I am not a lawyer. The information in this chapter does not constitute legal advice in a professional sense. Also remember that the stories I am about to relate to you do not reflect current legal climates, but experiences that occurred as long as a decade ago. To understand my theory on how to be a happy, homeschooling mother, you need to know a little about my background.

In chapter 1, I told you how I became a homeschooler. The school district would not allow me to hold my oldest son back, even though we had extensive and expensive testing done to verify what I knew to be true: he just wasn't ready for first grade. By the time the school district notified me of their refusal to let me begin Ty a year late, all the private schools I would have considered sending him to were filled, ruling out the option of private schools. When I threatened to homeschool, school district personnel acted almost nonchalant about it. "Go ahead; the school board has gotten lenient with that kind of thing," they told me.

I had no information as to how to become a legal homeschooler. I was forced to hire an attorney to find out what South Carolina law required of homeschooling families in 1984. There were no support groups or state organizations to call on for information, advice, or support. I had to dig up my own information. I spent eight weeks in intensive research. I took a crash course in early childhood education. In July, I finally submitted an application to homeschool to my local school board, over thirty pages in all. (There were no alternatives to school district supervision in South Carolina at the time.)

Even though I had complied with the law, the school board denied my application to homeschool because I was not a certified teacher (which was not a requirement of the law). I was not allowed to be present at the school board meeting where they denied my application. Now, I would never let that happen; then, I didn't know better.

When I opened the letter of rejection from the school board, I felt physically ill. This was July of 1984. Private schools were filled, the school district would not allow me to hold Ty back, and now they had denied my request to homeschool. What was I to do? My only option was to appeal the decision to the State Board of Education, which meant once again hiring an attorney and walking through another humiliating experience for which I had no preparation.

I could not believe that this was happening to me in the United States of America. My only crime was being an involved, committed parent. I thought surely if I could explain the situation rationally to someone in authority, he would understand and alleviate the problem. I paid a visit to the State Department of Education and asked to see the state superintendent of education. He graciously agreed to see me. I explained the situation to him as calmly as I could. His response was equally calm, "Well, Mrs. Tyler, you know you can be put in jail for truancy." (Through no fault of my own, the State Board meeting to vote on my request had been postponed until mid-September, when school had already been in session some three weeks. By that time, Ty would have missed more than the allowed absences; hence, the charges of truancy.) I didn't know then what the basis for his threat was. I was too scared to ask, but in spite of my fear I heard myself responding, "Well, you'll have to put me in jail."

I left the State Department reeling. Not only had I not wanted to homeschool, now I was going to be put in jail for it! The entire situation seemed like a nightmare careening totally out of control.

Until this point in time only two people in the world knew of my intentions to homeschool: my husband and my sister. My sister kept my children for me to attend the first homeschooling seminar in Atlanta, featuring Dr. and Mrs. Raymond S. Moore as the keynote speakers. I found Dr. Moore immediately and poured out my heart to him. He graciously listened and offered his support and assistance. We had many telephone conversations after that, with Dr. Moore ready to fly to Columbia and testify on my behalf if it became necessary. I will never forget his kindness to me. At the seminar I did meet a few other homeschooling families from South Carolina. Most of them were so scared that they would not put their names and phone numbers in writing, even for other homeschoolers!

With this new threat of jail, I had no choice but to tell my parents of my homeschooling plans. We have always been an extremely close family, and my parents have always been supportive. But, I thought this latest adventure of mine would be too much to bear even for the most forbearing of parents. When I went by my parents' home to level with them, my conversation went something like this: "Daddy, Mom, I'm going to homeschool Ty. I don't want to talk about it. Here's the literature, the research I've done, and my application to the school board. The

school board denied my request, so now I have to appeal
to the State Board of Education. My hearing is next week
and they've threatened to put me in jail. I didn't want you
to read about it in the papers." With that "thorough"
explanation, I ran out of their home and drove to my
home in a semi-hysterical state.

The next day, in his capacity as chairman of the board
at Baptist Medical Center, Columbia, my dad happened
to be sharing the podium at a speaking engagement with
Nancy Thurmond, wife of South Carolina Sen. Strom
Thurmond. He mentioned to her that I had contacted
the senator's office for a letter of recommendation and
had received no reply. After the senator's staff reviewed
the situation and realized that I had complied with the
law, Senator Thurmond met with Superintendent Williams on my behalf and provided him with a letter of
recommendation.

Senator Thurmond is a legend in South Carolina,
and his opinions carry great weight. After his intervention on my behalf, the State Board of Education decided
to overturn the local school board's ruling that had denied me the right to homeschool. This ended a six-month
nightmare that left me exhausted and frightened in its
wake.

The State Board handed down its decision in mid-
September. While we rejoiced at the news of their ruling,
I was still filled with apprehension and fear. I knew I
would be scrutinized during the course of the year. I had
made people angry when I applied to homeschool and
when I appealed the decision to the State Board. I never
quite knew what was waiting around the corner for me.

This experience was just the beginning of years spent
in courtrooms and the legislature. Time does not permit
me to share most of the experiences we have had as a
family, each one strengthening us for the next round.
There is one more story I will share with you before we
move on.

We have now journeyed in time from the fall of 1984

to the winter of 1991. I began SCAIHS in July of 1990, knowing we would most certainly end up in court, but not expecting it for a year or two. By February 1991, eleven SCAIHS families had been charged with truancy, a negative attorney general's opinion had been rendered regarding the legal validity of SCAIHS, and the legal counsel for the State Department of Education had sent out a memo to all ninety-one school districts notifying them that homeschoolers going through SCAIHS were not legal. As founder and president of SCAIHS, my name was synonymous with SCAIHS. Things did not look promising to say the least!

During this time period the following episode occurred. The children and I were having a quiet school morning when I looked out the window and saw two policemen approaching my front door. Given the tension surrounding homeschooling and SCAIHS, being taken to court and/or arrested were neither inconceivable nor unanticipated. Ty was age thirteen and very mature. I called him into the kitchen, told him to take John, age ten, and Elizabeth, age four, into the schoolroom, lock the door, and close the shades. I didn't want Lizzie to see me handcuffed and carried off in a police car. Then, I told Ty not to come out until we were gone, and then to call Papa (my dad)—as an attorney he would know what to do. Ty said, "Don't worry, Mom. God will take care of all of us, including you."

Before I opened the door, I got on my knees and prayed for my children. I had experienced so much hostility from the educational establishment that I was not surprised by any actions. The thing I feared most was not jail, but my children being removed from my home. God made me come face to face with my greatest fear, and I knew that no matter what happened He would take care of my children. It was a liberating moment.

The policeman banged at the door. "Ma'am, would you please step out on the porch; it seems we've got a little problem."

The officers asked me a few trivial questions, which to me seemed to take an eternity. Then, finally, one of the officers said, "Ma'am, we don't mean to scare you, but there's been a robbery in your neighborhood; we think the thieves ditched that old piece of junk in front of your house (pointing to an old car to the front and side of the house), and they may even be in your backyard."

Criminals in the backyard I could handle! I was so relieved that they were not there for me, all I could say was, "Praise God!" The policemen looked at me like I was truly crazy, and I was glad that the children were in the schoolroom with the doors locked and the shades down. (The old piece of junk that the policemen had referred to was our second car—a nineteen-year-old Cutlass my dad had given me in high school, but it truly was a piece of junk at that point in time.) The police were thoroughly disgusted that their theory had been blown. They told me to be careful, and "tell that husband of yours to buy you a new car!"

Back inside the sanctuary of my own home, I didn't know whether to laugh or cry. So, I did a little of both. I do not want any homeschooling mother to experience the things I did. Homeschooling can be difficult enough without the added stresses and expense of legal problems and threats.

As a homeschooling mother, I view legal preparedness in homeschooling in much the same way that I view safety belts. You wear your safety belt every time you're in the car, with the hope that you will never need it. At age four, my son John announced to his grandfather to always wear his seat belt because seat belts prevent wrecks! After a good laugh, we were able to explain to John that seat belts are not a preventative, but they do allow us to face wrecks with a greater chance of healthy survival.

Statistically, most people will never be involved in a wreck; but for those who are, the expense and inconvenience of safety belts, air bags, and antilock brakes are inconsequential compared to the avoidance or minimization of injury or the saving of a life. Most of us as homeschooling parents will never have to face a truant officer or a Department of Social Services worker. However, percentages are not comforting when you become the one that encounters difficulties. Legal problems in homeschooling can involve a minor bump-up or a head-on collision. In either case, your safety, as well as your children's safety, may well depend on the precautions you have taken ahead of time. When you see the wreck coming, it's too late to buckle your seat belt. Everyone needs to be legally prepared before he begins homeschooling.

Situations differ from family to family. Some may be considering homeschooling seriously but leisurely. We get calls in our office weekly from mothers of infants and toddlers who are considering homeschooling and want to be prepared when the time comes.

You have plenty of time to understand the constitutional issues undergirding homeschooling, important court cases, and the laws in your own state. You have time to become connected with local support group leaders and members to learn the ropes in your particular locale. This is ideal.

Many of us do not have this luxury when we begin to homeschool. We often hear from parents whose children have attended public or private schools happily for years. An incidence of violence, the introduction of Outcome-Based Education in the classroom, or inexplicable unhappiness in a child may force them to consider the homeschooling alternative. In this situation, time is of the essence. You need answers swiftly.

Legal Basis for Homeschooling

You need to be armed with the facts concerning your legal basis for homeschooling as an American citizen. This includes knowledge of the United States Constitution and Bill of Rights, Supreme Court decisions, your state constitution, and your state's homeschooling statute.

The highest law in the land is the United States Constitution, followed by the fifty state constitutions. The word *education* does not appear in the entire context of the United States Constitution, but two amendments in the Bill of Rights have direct bearing on the right of parents to direct the education of their children.

The text of the First Amendment is as follows:

> Congress shall make no law respecting an establishment of religion, or prohibiting the free exercise thereof; or abridging the freedom of speech, the press; or the right of the people peaceably to assemble, and to petition the Government for a redress of grievances.

Section one of the Fourteenth Amendment reads as follows:

> All persons born or naturalized in the United States, and subject to the jurisdiction thereof, are citizens of the United States and the State wherein they reside. No State shall make or enforce any law which shall abridge the privileges or immunities of citizens of the United States; nor shall any State deprive any person of life, liberty, or property, without due process of law; nor deny to any person within its jurisdiction the equal protection of the laws.

For those who homeschool for religious reasons, implications of the First Amendment are obvious. The government cannot prohibit the free exercise of religion.

Supreme Court decisions have been instrumental in defining the role of the Fourteenth Amendment pertaining to issues of educational freedom. *Pierce v. Society of Sisters* (1925) rendered the state of Oregon powerless in its efforts to force all children to attend public schools.[1] The following statement from the *Pierce* decision is fraught with significance for homeschooling parents:

> The fundamental theory of liberty upon which all governments in this Union repose excludes any

power of the state to standardize its children by forcing them to accept instruction from public teachers only. The child is not a mere creature of the state; those who nurture and direct his destiny have the right, coupled with the high duty, to recognize and prepare him for additional obligations. (*Pierce*, 268 U.S. 510, 535)

As recently as 1979, the Supreme Court took the opportunity to strongly endorse parental rights in *Parham v. J. R.* (442 U. S. 584):[2]

Our jurisprudence historically has reflected Western civilization concepts of the family as a unit with broad parental authority over minor children. Our cases have consistently followed that course; our constitutional system long ago rejected the notion that a child is "the mere creature of the State" and, on the contrary, asserted that parents generally "have the right, coupled with the high duty, to recognize and prepare [their children] for additional obligations." (*Pierce v. Society of Sisters*, 268 U.S. 510, 535 [1925])

The law's concept of the family rests on a presumption that parents possess what a child lacks in maturity, experience, and capacity for judgment required for making life's difficult decisions. More important, historically it has been recognized that natural bonds of affection lead parents to act in the best interests of their children.

As with so many other legal presumptions, experience and reality may rebut what the law accepts as a starting point; the incidence of child neglect and abuse cases attests to this. That some parents "may at times be acting against the interests of their children" . . . creates a basis for caution, but is hardly a reason to discard wholesale those pages of human experience that teach that parents generally do act in the child's best interest . . . . The statist notion that governmental power should supersede

parental authority in all cases because some parents abuse and neglect children is repugnant to
American tradition.

Time does not allow us to devote adequate attention
to more fully construct the constitutional arguments supporting parents' rights to direct the education of their
children. For a fuller treatment of the subject, refer to
The Right Choice by Christopher Klicka, senior counsel for
Home School Legal Defense Association.

You may ask, and rightly so, If the Constitution clearly
preserves the right of parents to direct the education of
their children, isn't that the only legal knowledge and
protection we need? If the Constitution is clearly con-
strued to favor parental rights in education, why all the
hoopla about homeschooling and the law? Why must you
deal with local or state officials at all?

> During the first 250 years of the United States,
> beginning in 1620, education was not subject to the
> myriads of regulations which presently conflict with
> the parent's right to control the *process* of their
> children's education. Parental liberty was held in-
> violate, and parents seriously heeded the rights and
> responsibilities of educating their children. Educa-
> tion was *not* a government responsibility, and it was
> left completely under the private control of parents
> and the churches. . . . Until the 1900's the Chris-
> tian concept of parental liberty in education was
> unquestioned. . . . The problem, however, is that the
> Supreme Court, in the same breath in which it
> reasserted the parents' right to educate their chil-
> dren, also created an "interest" which the state has
> in education. Consequently, with this "interest" in
> education comes government controls.[3]

I would encourage you to read the Declaration of
Independence and the Constitution of the United States,
including the Bill of Rights. These are the defining documents of our country, but it is amazing how few adults

have actually read these. You also need to read your state constitution. Although the United States Constitution is silent on the topic of education, most state constitutions are not.

Once you understand the principles of liberty that are at stake when you begin to consider homeschooling, you must become familiar with the law(s) in your state governing homeschooling. If you will call Home School Legal Defense Association (address and phone number are found in appendix C), they will mail you a synopsis of the law in your state free of charge.

An invaluable resource at this point is your state homeschooling organization. They should be able to acquaint you with the law in your state and put you in touch with a local support group in your area. This becomes important because sometimes treatment of homeschoolers varies even within the same state. South Carolina has ninety-one autonomous school districts. Some are very supportive of homeschooling, while others have been openly hostile to the point of taking homeschooling families who have complied with the law to court. State leaders and/or local leaders can walk you through the process in your state. They can also inform you which school districts are friendly and which are not. They can tell you of legal alternatives to school district supervision, if any exist.

The following chart gives a very general overview of the homeschooling laws in the United States. Not all state laws are neatly or easily categorized, but, for your convenience, I have tried to keep the chart as simple as possible. For a full rendering of your state's law contact HSLDA or your state association. This chart is adapted from information found in *Home Schooling in the United States: A Legal Analysis* and is used with permission from Christopher Klicka.[4]

Summary of
Homeschool Laws in the Fifty States

Thirty-eight states have adopted homeschooling
statutes or regulations.

Alaska	New York
Arizona	North Carolina
Arkansas	Maryland
Colorado	New Mexico
Connecticut	North Dakota
Florida	Ohio
Georgia	Oklahoma
Hawaii	Oregon
Iowa	Pennsylvania
Louisiana	Rhode Island*
Maine*	South Carolina**
Massachusetts*	Tennessee
Minnesota	Utah*
Mississippi	Vermont
Missouri	Virginia
Montana	Washington
Nevada	West Virginia
New Hampshire	Wisconsin
New Jersey	Wyoming

*These states require homeschools to be subject to the discretionary "approval" of the local school district, school board, or state commissioner.

**South Carolina has two homeschooling statutes. Homeschoolers may join the South Carolina Association of Independent Home Schools (SCAIHS) in lieu of school district approval. Parents can also seek "approval" through their local school board. Approval is mandatory if all conditions of the law are met.

In at least fourteen states, homeschools may operate as private or church schools, under private or church schools, or as alternative instruction programs.

Alabama	Kansas
Alaska	Kentucky
California	Louisiana
Delaware	Michigan
Idaho	Nebraska
Illinois	South Dakota
Indiana	Texas

Forty states do not require homeschool parents to have any specific qualifications, but eight states require a high school diploma or GED.

Arizona	Ohio
Georgia	Pennsylvania
New Mexico	South Carolina
North Carolina	Tennessee

The remaining two states have a variety of qualification requirements. North Dakota requires the passage of a "teacher's test" or a college diploma. West Virginia allows parents with a GED or high school diploma to teach until a child reaches high school. West Virginia parents must remain four years ahead of the student.

Seven states require instruction or amount of time to be "equivalent" to public schools.

Connecticut	Maine
Indiana	Nevada
Iowa	New Jersey
Kansas	

The term *equivalent* was struck down by courts as void for vagueness in Minnesota and Montana.

Three states require instruction to be "regular" and thorough.

Delaware	Maryland	Rhode Island

Two states require instruction to be "comparable" to public schools.

Idaho   Michigan

Four states require homeschool teachers to be "competent," "qualified," or "capable of teaching."

California   New York
Kansas   Ohio

In four other states, groups of homeschoolers have qualified as private or church schools.

Colorado   Maine
Florida   Utah

In South Carolina, SCAIHS qualifies as an accrediting *association* as opposed to a school.

Twenty-nine states require standardized testing or evaluation.

Sixteen states require standardized testing.

Alaska   North Carolina
Arkansas   North Dakota
Georgia*   Oregon
Hawaii   Pennsylvania
Minnesota   South Carolina*
Nevada   South Dakota
New Mexico   Tennessee
New York   Washington*

*Georgia and Washington do not require submission of results to the public schools. SCAIHS members are not required to submit results to public schools.

Thirteen states provide an alternative to testing.

Colorado   Maine   Virginia
Connecticut   Massachusetts   Washington
Florida   New Hampshire   West Virginia
Iowa   Ohio
Louisiana   Vermont

Connecticut only requires a portfolio review. Colorado does not require submission of test results or evaluation to the public school.

Oklahoma is the only state with a constitutional amendment that specifically guarantees the right to homeschool.

Do not be discouraged or intimidated by the legal aspects of homeschooling. Remember that everyone has to start somewhere. The more you familiarize yourself with the legal issues surrounding homeschooling and the laws in your state, the more comfortable you will become. You do not need to be a legal expert—you just need to know enough to homeschool without fear.

When I began homeschooling, I was overwhelmed by the extent and the expense of my legal problems. The homeschooling community has come a long way! We have organized politically and legally. We have developed a formidable grassroots network—both on the state and national levels. One of the most significant organizations that has given homeschoolers staying power is Home School Legal Defense Association (HSLDA).

South Carolina has been one of the most litigious states in the union concerning homeschooling. To answer a burgeoning mound of legal problems in the mid-eighties, we lobbied intensively for two years for a homeschooling statute that would put an end to the litigation. To our dismay, the bill that was signed into law in 1988 had been so dramatically amended that it actually increased litigation rather than reducing it. The most onerous amendment was one that required all non-degreed parents to make a passing score on the Education Entrance Examination (EEE), a test designed for those entering the professional teaching field.

HSLDA filed a class-action lawsuit on behalf of its members in South Carolina. This case was lost at the trial court level and had to be appealed to the South Carolina Supreme Court, where HSLDA eventually won. If South

Carolina were allowed to implement teacher testing standards for homeschooling parents, it could have set a dangerous precedent by ushering in a new wave of parent-teacher regulation nationwide. Michael Farris, president of HSLDA, perceiving the threat not only to South Carolinians but others as well, attacked the study that had been conducted to validate the use of the EEE with homeschooling parents. Mike brought in expert witnesses from across the country, including one of the country's leading testing experts. At one point, the state of South Carolina ran out of money and could no longer take depositions, but the HSLDA staff was like the Energizer Bunny—they kept going and going and going. HSLDA's victory reaped benefits for homeschoolers far beyond the bounds of South Carolina.

In 1991, SCAIHS was the plaintiff in one lawsuit and the defendant in another, with HSLDA serving as our legal counsel in both cases. We lost both of the trial court cases and appealed both decisions to the state supreme court. Before either case could be tried at the Supreme Court, representatives from the State Department of Education contacted me to find out if there was a way to forego the litigation and solve the "homeschooling problem" in South Carolina. (The judge in one of the lawsuits had declared this to be an issue that should be solved in the legislature, rather than in the courts. Both parties agreed that we should take the judge's admonition to heart.)

As one state employee told me, "Usually we say 'boo' and groups like yours go scattering like scared mice. But you have staying power because you have good legal representation." Litigation in South Carolina has been the nudge the establishment needed to find a fair and equitable way to deal with homeschooling families in our state. As a relatively small homeschooling community at the time, there is no way we could have financed the sustained legal pressure that eventually brought resolution to our problems.

I have been through legal proceedings on my own. It was like going through surgery with no anesthesia. Like surgery, no legal proceedings are ever minor if they happen to you, but the pain is greatly reduced by being supported and represented by the kind and caring staff of HSLDA. In addition, you face *no* bills when the proceedings are over. Your only cost is one hundred dollars per year, or eighty-five dollars if you qualify for the group discount. You can easily pay more than one-hundred dollars per *hour* for good legal representation today. As Gregg Harris says, "Home School Legal Defense Association—Don't stay home without it."[5] (See appendix C for a fuller explanation of HSLDA.)

HSLDA membership is a requirement for membership in SCAIHS. I know from personal, painful experience that you don't have to be guilty to be taken to court. One of our members was taken to family court in 1994, even though she was in full compliance with South Carolina's compulsory attendance law. We had demonstrated her compliance to the local school district, the solicitor, and the Department of Social Services to no avail. To top it all off, this mother worked on a part-time basis for an attorney in her hometown. She was still taken to court. This is the letter she sent to the SCAIHS staff after the ordeal was over.

> Dear Zan:
>
> I'm at a loss for words to express my sincere appreciation for SCAIHS and for you! I don't think I would have made it through the fiasco in November at the County Family Court without your support. . . . I also want to laud the Home School Legal Defense Association. I was truly impressed with Dee Black and David Gordon. I was amazed that this association would send not only one but two highly qualified attorneys from out-of-state to represent my daughter and me in a hearing that was unnecessary, but could not be dismissed without a court appearance according to our "efficient"

bureaucracy of social workers and assistant solici-
tors. This was in spite of the fact that they each and
every one had been supplied with supporting documentation that my daughter was not under their
jurisdiction.

I know that you have had homeschooling parents
who have had questions about why they have to pay
extra money to join HSLDA when the state law so
clearly allows homeschooling under the SCAIHS
statute. I questioned it myself. Now I know! The
membership fee we pay to HSLDA is quite a bar-
gain when you consider what an attorney with the
distinct specialty of homeschooling, his transportation and other expenses of traveling from near
Washington, D.C. would cost on an hourly basis—
much less two highly experienced attorneys.

I really appreciate your calling to check on my
daughter and me that next evening.

God bless you all.

Membership in HSLDA is a deterrent to legal problems. It is the nature of bureaucracy and government to
take advantage of the little guy or the weak link. No one
ever picks on my seven-year-old daughter—not because
she inspires fear and trembling, but because they know
they are going to have to answer to two protective, big
brothers if they do. In much the same way, membership
in HSLDA is a bully deterrent. It is also a safety measure—like putting on your safety belt when you enter an
automobile. It may protect you when you are least expecting an accident.

One reason anyone can homeschool today is due in
part to the major contributions Home School Legal Defense Association has made in the legal arena of parental
rights. By making very affordable legal protection available, anyone can homeschool with peace of mind.

Another important advocacy group for homeschooling
families is the Rutherford Institute, whose founder and

president is John Whitehead. One of the five areas of constitutional rights to which Rutherford is committed to defend is homeschooling. If you experience legal problems while homeschooling, you can contact Rutherford. They will connect you with a legal assistant, who will help you in anyway he can. The Rutherford Institute decides which cases to take on a case-by-case basis. (See appendix C.)

Legal fears can rob you of your joy in homeschooling; don't let that happen to you. If you know just a fraction of what is in this chapter, you know more now than I did twelve years ago when I began homeschooling. Taking the time to acquaint yourself with the legal issues surrounding homeschooling will make you more confident in what you are doing now and in the future.

Chapter Four

How Can I Build a Support Network?

Anyone can homeschool, but you must decide for yourself whether homeschooling is for you and your family. I am a homeschooling mother and a homeschooling advocate. I have lobbied for homeschooling, spoken about homeschooling, written about homeschooling, and have been prosecuted and persecuted for homeschooling. But, I do not want to pressure anyone into making the decision to homeschool. Why? Homeschooling is a commitment—a big commitment. And, like anything in this world worth doing, it carries a price.

Only God is omniscient. Only He knows all the circumstances in your life. You should gather all the information you can about homeschooling, study it, and reach a decision in the quietness of your own home—or at least in your own heart. Don't make the decision to homeschool at a convention surrounded by hundreds or thousands of enthusiasts. Don't decide to homeschool because everyone in your church is. In the midst of difficult or discouraging days, you need to know that you made this decision. Succumbing to pressures from others will only lead to bitterness when the road gets a little rocky.

I encourage everyone who is contemplating homeschooling to arrange a day away from the children to seek God's guidance. I realize this can be a monumental effort, but it will reap great dividends in the end. For many,

homeschooling is an easy decision and one they made
when their children were born; for others it becomes the
most agonizing of decisions. Regardless of which situation fits you, you will benefit from some extended time
alone with the Lord. After eleven years of homeschooling,
I still follow this practice; only now I try to take out two
days a year—one before the school year begins, and one
at the midyear point.

When I made the decision to homeschool twelve years
ago, I knew no one who homeschooled. I had only one
book on homeschooling, *Homegrown Kids* by Dr. and Mrs.
Raymond Moore. Not only were there no homeschooling
conventions like every state has now, I couldn't find a
publisher to sell me a teacher's manual for my son's K-5
program. I finally ended up with a teacher's manual I
purchased on the "black market." There was no state
organization, and there were no local support groups. I
had no teen-age homeschooled students to observe to
assuage my fears—and everyone else's—concerning socialization. And, at the age of twenty-eight, having made
the decision to homeschool only two months prior, I was
threatened with jail.

I was frightened—scared to death is more like it—
and intimidated. But, I remembered something that my
Young Life leader used to tell me in high school: "Never
doubt in the darkness what God has shown you in the
light." I had spent days in fasting and prayer, seeking
God's guidance for my son. My turmoil increased as I
pondered the advantages and disadvantages of the public
and Christian schools; but my internal turmoil ended as
I considered the homeschooling option. The Lord used
several Scripture passages to lead and direct me. The
first was Proverbs 3:5–6:

> Trust in the Lord with all your heart,
> And do not lean on your own understanding.
> In all your ways acknowledge Him,
> And He will make your paths straight.

The second was several passages from Hebrews 11:

> Now faith is the assurance of things hoped for, the conviction of things not seen. (vs. 1)

> And without faith it is impossible to please Him, for he who comes to God must believe that He is, and that He is a rewarder of those who seek Him. (vs. 6)

> By faith Noah, being warned by God about things not yet seen, in reverence prepared an ark for the salvation of his household. (vs. 7)

> By faith Abraham, when he was called, obeyed by going out to a place which he was to receive for an inheritance; and he went out, *not knowing where he was going*. (emphasis mine, vs. 8)

I viewed homeschooling as my ark. I found myself identifying with Noah and the ridicule he must have suffered as he built this ark; but Noah loved God and his family more than the approval of man. I love the quote from a homeschooling newsletter in Luanne Shackelford's and Susan White's book *A Survivor's Guide to Homeschooling*: "Homeschooling is like building an ark in your backyard, and hoping the neighbors won't notice!"[1]

I could also identify with Gideon, who several times in the course of his lifetime had to ask God, "If I have found favor in Thy sight, then show me a sign that it is Thou who speakest with me" (Judg. 6:17). Many times I have told the Lord that I will homeschool or continue to homeschool, as long as I know it is He who has spoken to me. I have clung to the words of the psalmist in Psalm 32:8–10:

> I will instruct you and teach you in the way which you should go;

> I will counsel you with my eye upon you.

> Do not be as the horse or as the mule which have no understanding,

Whose trappings include bit and bridle to hold
them in check,

Otherwise they will not come near to you.

Many are the sorrows of the wicked;

But he who trusts in the Lord, lovingkindness shall
surround him.

God promises that if we draw near to Him, He will
draw near to us. If we seek Him, we will find Him. The
great Baptist preacher Charles Hadden Spurgeon once
said that prayer is the rope by which we ring the bells of
heaven. Homeschooling has kept me pulling that rope
and ringing those bells. We ought to always pray and not
lose heart.

My dear pastor, the late Gary Aitken, used to tell the
story of the great Reformed evangelist George Whitfield
being questioned about the theology of Methodist John
Wesley. When asked once if Whitfield would see Wesley
in heaven, his response was this: "John Wesley will shine
so brightly in heaven, no one will notice me."

Only you can know if God is calling you to homeschool.
No one else can or should make that determination for
you. I have many, many friends whose children are in
public, private, or Christian schools who will "shine much
more brightly in heaven than I." Many of these same
folks are better parents than I. That is not the issue. The
question is this: What is God leading you to do? The only
way to answer that question is to humble yourself before
God, commit your way to Him, and trust in His
lovingkindness to lead you and keep you. Therefore, I
commend you to Him alone who holds the keys to knowledge and wisdom.

I believe that God has called me to marriage and to
motherhood every bit as much as He has called my pastor to preach. Homeschooling has been a vehicle through
which I have endeavored to implement the charge of
Titus 2 in my home—to love my husband and to love my
children. Homeschooling is not an end in itself; it is a
means to an end.

Why have I included all of this in a chapter on building a support network? External support is important, but it may not always be there. Homeschooling my children has been one of my life's most rewarding experiences. To say that it has always, or ever, been easy would be a misrepresentation of my life. When the trials come, I can persevere because I know it is God who has called me. If I did not have the assurance of God's call in my life, trials would become barriers rather than instruments of sanctification.

Write It Down!

I encourage every homeschooling parent to write down his/her reasons for homeschooling. This becomes your philosophy of education. If you have scriptural reasons for homeschooling, write them down. Commit to writing your other reasons for homeschooling. As your children grow older and as you homeschool longer, your reasons may change. Write it down. Committing an idea to writing helps us define our thoughts and our goals. Thoughts can often be nebulous and fleeting and remain that way until we write them down. You do not have to be a scholar or published author to benefit from the defining process of writing. On difficult days, refer to those reasons to maintain your vision, inspiration, and sense of purpose.

Husbands and Wives

Some husbands and wives go through the decision-making process together. Many times a wife will want to homeschool, but the husband is a little skeptical. My husband, Joe, was in this camp. He is a very discerning person, who is never tempted to jump on anyone's band wagon. Nor does he seem to be subject to peer pressure (including mine!) or other people's opinions. When we began homeschooling, he agreed to it because he trusts my judgment. He was not totally convinced that homeschooling was the way to go, but he knew how carefully I had researched the options and knew how much I love the children. Today he admits another key factor in his decision was he did not think I could ruin Ty's education by homeschooling him in kindergarten! In the past eleven years we have grown together in our commitment to homeschool our children. Joe has the opportunity to counsel with many husbands who have the same reservations he had eleven years ago.

If your husband is adamantly opposed to homeschooling, appeal to him; make your case to him; ask God to change his heart. But, don't homeschool without at least having his acquiescence. Many husbands say, "We'll try it for a year." That's fine, but if your husband is really against it, don't do it. Your marriage comes first. You will need your husband's support in the homeschooling venture. Homeschooling for the first time can bring stresses of its own; you certainly do not want to add marital discord to the equation. Very few people can manage to keep a *Better Homes and Garden* house while homeschooling. A supportive husband pitches in and helps, or at least keeps his complaints to himself. A husband who does not want you homeschooling in the first place will probably not be pleased when science projects engulf the house or dinner is late.

A word of warning is in order at this point. Many mothers who become interested in homeschooling tend to devour every book and magazine available on the topic. The husband usually (not always, of course) has less time to read. Many homeschool authors and leaders advocate particular lifestyles in addition to homeschooling. This is not wrong. However, we need to remember that authors (present company included) and leaders are human beings subject to error. Read with discernment. Do not be afraid to disagree with what you read. Only the Bible is infallible.

Remember that your responsibility is to your spouse, not to an author. Discuss lifestyle changes together. Don't try to change your lifestyle without thoroughly discussing the ideas and/or changes you want to make with your spouse. The marriage relationship is sacred. Guard it jealously. Homeschooling is a vehicle that should enhance and strengthen your family life a hundredfold. Don't let bondage to someone else's ideas destroy your joy. Don't be afraid of change and even sacrifice, but make sure you are responding to God's leading and not an individual who has no God-given authority in your life. Many books contain good ideas; some even contain inspiring, life-changing ideas. Just remember you are married to your spouse—not a book!

Extended Family

Although it does not always happen, it is wonderful when extended family supports your decision to homeschool. If your parents or in-laws are receptive, give them information on homeschooling that shows both the successes and benefits. Involve them in your homeschool. One of the priceless benefits for me has been the extended time my children have been able to spend with my parents and Joe's parents. We are blessed to have four supportive grandparents who love our children and have been willing to share themselves and their time. They have each impacted our children's lives in a unique way. They have also been an important source of support for me. They have watched the children, provided transportation, taken them shopping, and a myriad of other things. My dad has even been my public-relations advisor and my political liaison.

If you have no family in your area, pray and ask the Lord to send you an older couple to be involved in the lives of your children. Some churches sponsor "Adopt-a-grandparent" programs. This is a two-way street—you can be there for each other.

Local Support Groups

Local homeschooling support groups are of major importance to many homeschooling parents.[2] These groups can be formed based on geographic location, par-

ticular beliefs, teaching styles, or the ages of children.
Some churches even form support groups. You can usually obtain a list of local support groups through your
state homeschooling association. Services offered by these
support groups can be as diverse as the groups themselves. Most offer field trips for the children, meetings
for the moms (and sometimes dads), phone-trees to dis-
seminate legislative information, newsletters, and/or encouragement in general.

State Organizations

State organizations usually exist for the purpose of
networking the local support groups, publishing a newsletter, sponsoring an annual statewide convention, maintaining a presence at the state legislature, working on
state legislation when needed, and disseminating legislative information.[3] Some states have two or more state
organizations due to the different nature of the groups.
Where this is the case, it is extremely important that
these groups lay aside their differences when it comes to
legislative issues. The homeschooling community is not
large enough or powerful enough to support different
legislative agendas on the state level—that is the kiss of
death for both groups. Remember Lincoln's words: "A
house divided against itself cannot stand." I encourage
everyone to join your state organization. Usually the dues
are minimal, and they need your support to be effective.

National Organizations

National groups exist on a number of different fronts
and for different reasons. Some organizations provide
curriculum and correspondence courses, others provide
legal services, others provide a way for state leaders to
network, and still others maintain a presence on Capitol
Hill. For a listing of these, please refer to appendices C
and D.

First-Year Homeschoolers

Depending on your personality and your circumstances, first-year homeschoolers usually need support and encouragement. Your first year will be your most difficult in terms of adjustment and acclimating yourself to a new way of living. Don't be afraid to ask for help and seek the support you need. Find veteran homeschoolers to call upon. Don't expect to have it all together. Expect to make mistakes, and move on. Take joy in your family, and for goodness sake, don't compare yourself to someone who has been homeschooling for twenty-five years!

Remember, every child gets a first-year teacher sooner or later; just be thankful your child will have only one! Seriously, the energy and enthusiasm many first-year homeschoolers bring to the task more than compensates for a lack of experience.

Don't Forget the Church and Community

Sometimes as homeschooling parents, it is easy to get so wrapped up in our homes that we forget there is a needy world out there. Obviously, a mother with five preschoolers will have less time for others than a homeschooling mother whose children are grown and gone. We have seasons in life when we must focus totally on our families. However, if we view homeschooling properly, it can give us the freedom we need to concentrate some of our efforts on the needs of others. We can incorporate community involvement into our studies. We can incorporate needy families or individuals into our family life. The family can become a center of ministry that supports the church and the community. These efforts do not need to be monumental. Use your common sense. But as we look for ways to love our neighbors, I believe God will give us those opportunities. Homeschooling is a training ground, not a permanent residence. We want to train our children to love and serve both God and our fellow man.

A Word about Homeschooling
Special Needs Students

Entire volumes exist on teaching the child with special needs. It is impossible to do the topic justice in a few brief pages. My goal is simply to point you in the right direction: to acquaint you with available resources and encourage you in the task at hand. If you are the parent of a special needs child, you face hurdles that other parents do not—whether you are homeschooling or not. You may need more support and encouragement than the parents of other children. Special needs can include a variety of things: physical handicaps, visual impairment, hearing impairment, learning disabilities, attention deficit disorder, psychological handicaps, mental handicaps, or multiple handicaps.

Homeschooling can be extremely beneficial for special needs children. All of the advantages of homeschooling become of paramount importance with the special needs child. They, more than all other students, need an individualized education program (IEP), administered on a one-to-one basis. Although special education programs in traditional schools usually have a lower teacher-to-student ratio than regular classrooms, rarely are these children in an environment where they can receive constant one-on-one attention.

In an analysis of a recent study conducted by Dr. Steven Duvall, Dr. Brian Ray of the National Home Education Research Institute, makes the following observations:

> Dr. Steven Duvall compared the academic engaged time (AET) and basic skill development of learning disabled students who were home educated to those in public school special education programs. Higher rates of AET and greater academic gains were made by the home educated. "Parents, even without special education training, provided powerful instructional environments at home."[4]

At SCAIHS, the number of parents enrolling special needs children is growing exponentially each year. Linda Truax, M.Ed., is the consultant for students with special needs for SCAIHS. Linda herself was homeschooled in high school and, after teaching for years in both public and private schools, is teaching her own children at home. Linda has been certified as a therapist by the National Institute for Learning Disabilities; however, I think her most compelling credential is that she homeschools a special needs child of her own. In a recent conversation, Linda gave me the following advice for teaching a special needs student:

1. Remember that experts do not always know what is best for your child. Often what they prescribe is really a prescription for homeschooling.

2. These children need one-on-one teaching in small blocks of time, frequent breaks, constant review and repetition, and immediate feedback.

3. You don't necessarily need to use a different curriculum; learn how to adapt existing material to meet their needs and learning styles.

4. Remember that teaching a special needs child can be time-consuming and frustrating. This is true for the home educator and the classroom teacher alike. You don't get the fast results and the big strides in achievement that you see in other children. Oftentimes, depending on the severity of the child's problems, the results may touch your heart more than change the child's statistical achievement.

5. Do not compare your child to any other homeschooled child. Many homeschooling parents pride themselves in their children's high test scores. Do not let this discourage you. Also, don't compare your effectiveness as a teacher with the mother whose child is scoring in the 99th percentile.

6. Find other homeschooling parents in your area that deal with special needs. As the number of homeschooled special needs students grows, so do avail-

ability of support groups and special services. See appendix E for some resources available to parents of special needs children.

We received a letter at the SCAIHS office that describes the incredible progress that parents can make simply by teaching their special needs children at home:

Dear SCAIHS:

Thank you so much for being there! You have not only been a lifesaver, but a blessing from God for this family. You have been an encouragement. You have been support during a dark time. You have been the answer to my son's learning disabilities. We cannot express our appreciation enough.

After seven years in public education my son has finally read his first library book. Needless to say, this mother has shed tears of thankfulness over this accomplishment. I had almost given up when they told me what my son could never accomplish. He is learning at such a fast pace and is amazing us!

Again, thank you all so much and a special thanks to Linda. We do love you.

(Name Withheld)

A Word about Homeschooling High School Students

If there is anything more intimidating than homeschooling special needs students, it is homeschooling high school students. When we began SCAIHS just five years ago, we had a total of seven high school students. We finished the 1994–95 school year with right at two hundred high school students. This phenomenal growth mirrors the growth that is occurring nationwide at the high school level.

Homeschooling at the high school level can be done very successfully with careful thought and planning. As the success of homeschooling becomes more apparent, colleges and employers are anxious to tap into this source of potential students and employees.

> Even at top-level universities, the generally positive experiences with students who have been homeschooled are changing initial reservations administrators may have harbored about the capabilities of such students. "Our experience with the ones we have admitted has been very good," says David Illingworth, associate director of financial aid at Harvard University.[5]

In December of 1994, I had the opportunity to speak about homeschooling and the SCAIHS High School Program at the Annual Convention of the Carolinas Association of College Registrars and Admissions Officers. It was a time for me to acquaint them with the advantages of homeschooling, and for them to share with me what they are looking for in homeschooled high school students. They were thrilled to hear about our high school program because of the objective documentation we provide for each student. This seemed to be their biggest need: objective documentation that corroborates the subjective information provided by the parents.

After interviewing many college admissions officers, Elise Edson, director of the SCAIHS High School Program, compiled the following information:[6]

What Colleges Consider Important:

1. High School Record: Transcript—what courses the student has completed; Diploma from an accredited school or program or GED

2. GPA: Grades earned, as well as credits earned

3. Test Scores: SAT or ACT

4. Special Talents: Music, athletics, etc.

5. Essay (where required)

6. Letters of Recommendation and Alumni Legacy

7. Extracurricular Activities (including community service, work experience, and travel experiences)

8. Interview

9. Date of Application

Homeschooling in high school can be an exciting adventure. Students have time to develop serious academic interests as well as extracurricular ones. (See chapter 6, appendices A, and E for sources of high school curriculum and courses of study.) Parents are bringing great creativity to teaching upper-level high school courses. Some parents co-op, with each parent teaching the subject in which he is strongest. Some hire tutors to teach difficult subjects. Feeling totally inadequate to teach a foreign language, I have hired a neighbor who used to teach in high school (and who is a fluent speaker) to teach my boys Spanish I, II, and III. Many parents and homeschooling organizations are arranging homeschooled classes for some high school courses. The boys have attended a home-school biology class, complete with lab, to meet one of their lab science requirements. A retired science teacher, and homeschooling grandfather, taught the class. He will teach a chemistry class next year.

The aspect of homeschooling in high school that thrills me is the ability to capitalize on each student's interests. Ty is able to pursue his interest in government and politics by working as a senate page two afternoons a week. Both boys have been extremely active in political campaigns. They are both involved on highly competitive sports teams. They have both had the opportunity through the warm inclusiveness of others to travel to foreign countries. John is able to pursue piano. And, they both do quite a bit of public speaking with me. The exciting thing is that my boys' activities are not unusual. Homeschooling parents nationwide are brainstorming and creatively pursuing challenging involvements for their high school students.

As homeschooling at the high school level becomes more prominent, other opportunities are presenting themselves. Many public and private high schools are opening courses for homeschooled students that some parents might find difficult to teach. Many states are allowing the homeschooled students who so desire to participate in interscholastic activities. Many other states are actively pursuing these opportunities through legislation or court actions. In May of 1995 Tim Echols with Family Resource Network brought TeenPact to South Carolina.[7] This is an intensive one-week introduction to state government. The participants were required to do quite a bit of research before the week of TeenPact. The week consisted of approximately seven-hour days of working and learning at the State House. The students met with their senators and representatives, learned the principles of lobbying, studied and researched bills, heard from a myriad of elected officials, researched campaign disclosure forms, attended subcommittee and committee hearings, and learned how they should conduct themselves as Christian citizens. What a phenomenal opportunity!

The opportunities for homeschooled high school students abound. As parents and students, we must look for these opportunities and try to create those that don't yet exist. The sky is the limit! Opportunities for service abound. Opportunities for meaningful work experience abound. Survey your teen's interests and begin looking for those windows of opportunity that will enhance and change his/her life. Pray that God will guide you and your teen and open doors. He can do exceedingly beyond that which we ask or think!

Part II

by Terry Dorian, Ph.D.

Chapter Five

What about Socialization?

socialize v. 2. To fit for companionship with others; make sociable in attitude or manners. 3. To convert or adapt to the needs of society. socialization n.[1]

Many of us have discovered that when family members, friends, acquaintances, or strangers ask home educators the question, What about socialization? the more pressing question which they want us to answer is, How will your children become socially competent without having the advantage of interacting with their peers in a school setting? Other questions usually follow: How can you provide experiences for your children which will compensate for the ones they will miss by not attending public or private schools? How can you prepare your children for excellence without giving them access to the facilities, equipment, experienced teachers, sports, music and art programs, and social activities offered by educational institutions? Aren't you concerned that your children will become socially and culturally deprived by not attending school?

No meaningful discussion about socialization can occur until we answer three questions: 1) what is socialization from a biblical perspective? 2) how does positive and principled sociability differ from negative, self-centered sociability? 3) who should we seek as biblical role models for our children? May the Word of God touch our hearts as we cry out, "Turn away my eyes from looking at vanity, and revive me in Thy ways" (Ps. 119:37).

The significance of socialization as defined by the *American Heritage Dictionary of the English Language* seems—on the surface—to be something we can easily grasp. All of us want to be fit companions—but for whom? In the present age, fit companions are not defined by biblical standards, but rather by the beliefs, attitudes, and values of endless numbers of groups and individuals. Television talk show hosts present a wide range of standards for behavior which are considered fit by those who dominate and control the mass media. Evil behavior and conversation are neither defined as such, nor censored; virtue is seldom recognized or encouraged. As decadence and wickedness of every sort is celebrated through the mass media, unprincipled men and women become the role models for millions of people, young and old, in America.

And, what about good manners and friendly attitudes? We are currently living under the oppression of the political correctness movement. Politically correct people reject, ridicule, ignore, and persecute people who insist that there are moral absolutes based on the inerrant Word of God; they tolerate, embrace, condone, and celebrate people who insist that there are no moral absolutes and who support their agenda. Good manners and friendly attitudes do not prevail when politically correct people are confronted by people whose standards of virtue are defined by the Word of God. In contemporary American society, there is no consensus regarding appropriate attitudes. As a result of the movement called political correctness, many teachers and students are ostracized and even suspended for discussing the relevance of traditional Western concepts. Christians in our society must constantly ask themselves: To whose society should we adapt? In this cultural war, Christians must resist being socialized by powerful anti-Christian forces. Politically correct people call white black and black white and redefine basic terms and concepts. Multiculturalists promote an understanding and appreciation of world culture which does not allow for the study and celebration of traditional Western concepts. The political correctness movement is changing our schools and using our schools as instruments of political indoctrination. Many parents decide to educate their children at home or to enroll them in private institutions in order to resist this kind of indoctrination. Institutions such as Hillsdale College in Hillsdale, Michigan, are publishing reference materials that will help parents, teachers, and educators to stand against the assault on the Judeo-Christian tradition. When parents order a reference guide, they receive a letter which begins as follows:

> As parents, teachers and educators, you join those modern-day pioneers who strive to reform the current educational agenda to which our nation has fallen victim. Because it is designed to foster a value-centered education among children ages five through thirteen, we trust that you will find the reference guide to be an indispensable part of daily instruction.[2]

Very often, Christians must consciously resist being socialized; we do not want to be fit companions for those who are foolish, overbearing, and intolerant. The behaviors and attitudes which unprincipled people deem appropriate are not ones to which we would unreservedly subscribe.

And, what about the needs of society? As Christians, we know that our society needs hard-working, thrifty, honest, generous, and kind-hearted people. The mass media presents as successful those who are hedonistic, deceitful, and mean-spirited. The immorality and violence in our educational institutions mirror the popular culture. William Bennett, who served as director of the Office of National Drug Control Policy under President Bush and as secretary of education under President Reagan expresses the dilemma in the March 1995 issue of *Commentary*: "We live in a culture which seems dedicated to the corruption of the young, to assuring the loss of their innocence before their time."[3]

The groups at war in our society define the needs of society according to their belief-attitude-value systems. As Christians, we have no trouble determining what our society needs; the Word of God clearly explains the need and tells us the way in which Christ answers the need in the lives of those who trust Him. Oftentimes, we as Christians must choose not to meet the perceived needs of society. Organizations such as Toward Tradition have taken a stand against those who are at war against traditional values. The programs and policies outlined by those who seek to undermine the Judeo-Christian tradition, are programs and policies which meet the needs of society, as the politically correct perceive them. The mission statement issued by Toward Tradition expresses what many of us believe to be our society's real and urgent need: "Toward Tradition unites Christians and Jews to restore the Judeo-Christian ethical tradition as the foundation of our culture, our economy and our political life."[4]

When Christians discuss socialization with other believers, the term itself may be useful. The term is helpful so long as we distinguish positive, principled sociability from negative, self-centered sociability. But, in the absence of such distinctions, *sociability* is defined by whatever belief, attitude, and value system prevails.

The Record of Western Civilization and Our Christian Heritage

In 1958, before the political correctness movement came to power, Harper and Brothers released a book entitled *In God We Trust, The Religious Beliefs and Ideas of the American Founding Fathers.* Norman Cousins, then-editor of *The Saturday Review*, selected, edited, and commented on the words written by these men; he made his selections after examining thousands of letters, personal diaries, and personal pronouncements. In *The Good In-*

heritance, a book he wrote twenty years earlier, he explored the fall of the Athenian civilization and discussed how the American Founding Fathers gained insight from the Athenian experience and profited from history in general. These insightful books are out of sync with today's political correctness movement, a movement which carefully defines appropriate speech and thought. And yet, these books define the attitudes and behaviors which thoughtful, virtuous people have deemed fit for centuries in the Western world. Not only must we refuse to be socialized by this movement; we must make the reason for our stand so very clear that even the unsuspecting among us may be able to resist the plans and programs of those who are redefining the meaning of virtue in America.

The words of our Founding Fathers remind us that America was founded by virtuous men with great ideas. As we read their letters, diaries, and proclamations, we are reminded that our very freedom exists because they based their lives on the authenticity of Scripture. As recently as 1958, most Americans still acknowledged the greatness of our Christian heritage. Now we have allowed the few who are in positions of power to rewrite history and to deny the relevance of our heritage. Our government, like no other, was founded on the best thinking in the history of Western civilization; ours is a government founded on a faith in the true and living God.

We now have a very different government, one with laws and opinions about laws which reveal a hostility to the Word of God. As those who are hostile to the Word of God seek to reorganize American society, we must preserve the historical record in order that we may remember who we are as a people. The record of Western civilization and the history of America are of great significance in the socialization process. George Washington and John Adams had no difficulty in defining and encouraging fit behavior; they based their definitions on the Word of God, and the entire country supported their leadership. Books such as *In God We Trust* challenge us to seek out the original documents and to publish and distribute them widely; because primary sources offer us evidence that God once blessed this country in a unique and miraculous way. The words of these great men remind us to seek wise companions, those whose goals are consistent with the Word of God; they challenge us to demand leadership which God can once again bless. Perhaps, we might answer the question, What about socialization? in this way: A Christian should adapt to the genuine needs of society by upholding the truth of God's Word. Only God can send revival, and many of us believe that He will; and, as we adapt to society in ways that are pleasing to God, we will win the lost to Christ without losing our children. The unwise adapt to society by being indoctrinated and absorbed.

The general orders of George Washington, written from the headquarters at Valley Forge, 2 May 1778 grip our hearts when we realize the incredible faith and virtue that once dominated our land!

> While we are zealously performing the duties of good Citizens and Soldiers we certainly ought not to be inattentive to the higher duties of Religion. To the distinguished Character of Patriot, it should be our highest Glory to add the more distinguished Character of Christian. The signal Instances of providential Goodness which we have experienced and which have now almost crowned our labours with complete success, demand from us in a peculiar manner the warmest returns of Gratitude and Piety to the Supreme Author for all Good.[5]

Other excerpts from the general orders of George Washington give us cause to celebrate as well:

> The blessing and protection of heaven are at all times necessary but especially so in times of public distress and danger—the General hopes and trusts, that every soldier and man will endeavor to so live, and act, as becomes a Christian Soldier defending

the dearest Rights and Liberties of his country. (Headquarters, New York, 9 July 1776)[6]

... that the troops may have an opportunity of attending public worship, as well as take some rest after the great fatigue they have gone through; The General in future excuses them from fatigue duty on Sundays (except at Ship Yards, or special occasions) until further orders. The General is sorry to be informed that the foolish, and wicked practice, of profane cursing and swearing (a Vice heretofore little known in an American Army) is growing into fashion; he hopes the officers will, by example, as well as influence, endeavor to check it, and that both they, and the men will reflect, that we can have little hopes of the blessing of Heaven on our Arms, if we insult it by our impiety, and folly; added to this, it is a vice so mean and low, without any temptation, that every man of sense, and character, detests and despises it. (Headquarters, New York, 3 August 1776)[7]

Just as George Washington's admonitions are timeless, so are John Adams's dreams of a perfect commonwealth. As we read his reflections about the kind of society which he believed would be a paradise, we can take heart in the fact that one of our Founding Fathers desired His will as the highest good. Throughout the New Testament, we are urged to seek just such a life as John Adams describes:

Suppose a nation in some distant region would take the Bible for their only law-book, and every member should regulate his conduct by the precepts there exhibited! Every member would be obliged, in conscience, to temperance and frugality and industry; to justice and kindness and charity towards his fellow men; and to piety, love and reverence towards Almighty God. In this commonwealth, no man would impair his health by gluttony, drunkenness, or lust; no man would sacrifice

his most precious time to cards or any other trifling
and mean amusement; no man would steal, or lie,
or in any way defraud his neighbor, but would live
in peace and good will with all men; no man would
blaspheme his Maker or profane his worship; but a
rational and manly, a sincere and unaffected piety
and devotion would reign in all hearts. What a
Utopia; what a Paradise would this region be! (John
Adams's personal diary, 22 February 1756)[8]

Discipleship Is the Goal of the Christian

When we as Christians seek to socialize our children,
our goal is to lead them to a knowledge of God; that they
may love Him, love their neighbor, and understand biblical principles. The Word of God offers us the way in
which we may know Him; but we can only understand the
Word by the power of the Spirit. We learn to know Him
by His grace, through faith in His Word. The Word reveals how we may become socially competent in Him: we
may have the fruit of the spirit (Gal. 5:22); we can know
what it is to be alive in Christ (Eph. 2:1–18); the whole
armor of God offers us complete protection (Eph. 4:17–
32); we may put on a new self which is in the likeness of
God (Eph. 4:17–32). As believers we can rest in Him,
looking to the integrity exemplified by the Apostle Paul
in 2 Corinthians 1:12. By God's grace and mercy may we
be able to speak the Apostle's word to our children:

> For our proud confidence is this, the testimony of
> our conscience, that in holiness and godly sincerity,
> not in fleshly wisdom but in the grace of God, we
> have conducted ourselves in the world, and espe-
> cially toward you. (2 Cor. 1:12)

We have the privilege of knowing and discipling our
children in a unique and wonderful way when we allow
our children to participate fully in our lives. By living
transparently before them, with unbridled affection, our
children rest in the absolute certainty of our love. But, in

order for children and young people to participate fully in our lives, we must allow them to see and to understand many of the choices which we face, while we are facing them. The Holy Spirit shows us when and how to reveal our questions as we look to God for the answers. Children need to see us work through certain areas of our lives again and again. They will learn dependency on God as they see our dependency on Him; they will learn faith as we celebrate victories together. If we pray together, confess our faults one to another, and trust the Lord, He will lead us through one step at a time. Every crisis is an opportunity for our children to watch our faith grow and to grow in faith themselves. As parents we must ask ourselves the basic questions and be certain that our children understand the answers:

How do we use the resources which God has given us?

How do we decide how to spend our time and money?

How do we develop relationships with other people?

Are we as parents servants to each other and to our children?

Are we slaves to our appetites, or are we under the control of the Holy Spirit in every area?

Do we enjoy close fellowship with the Lord?

Is praise and worship a natural part of our lives?

Do we respond to the Word with excitement and joy?

What do we do when we experience grief, loss, or disaster?

What do we do when our children disappoint us?

What do we do when we disappoint them?

How do we overcome fear, sorrow, anger, jealousy, greed, discontentment, and idolatry?

These questions are answered in the hearts of our children as we open our lives to them moment by moment, day by day, and hour by hour. Trust, time, and the spirit of Almighty God are essential in building interpersonal relationships which honor Christ. Few of us would place our trust in those who have no time for us, and yet, time is only the beginning. Only in Him do we know what to do with the time that He has given us.

Time often determines the very nature of relationships. Children are seldom able to participate fully in the lives of their friends at school or in the lives of their teachers. Casual and/or formal relationships do not give us the opportunities which family life allows to actually walk out the principles which we find in God's Word. The time which parents and siblings spend together hour by hour, day by day, in unbroken connection with each other provides an opportunity for trials and testing. In the course of a day, a week, a month, homeschooled children experience endless cycles of questions and conflicts which offer the opportunity for answers and resolutions. Almost anyone would agree that resolving conflict is an essential part of being socially competent. Parents who walk in the Spirit and not in the flesh, are able to disciple their children. This is God's plan for ending turmoil and strife. "For the flesh sets its desire against the Spirit, and the Spirit against the flesh; for these are in opposition to one another, so that you may not do the things that you please" (Gal. 5:17).

Most educators are fully convinced that schools provide an environment essential for socialization. Certainly, in very special Christian schools, in the presence of godly children and teachers, children may learn to walk by the Spirit. Such schools reinforce the godly principles which many of the children have learned in their homes. However, teaching students to love their neighbors as themselves is difficult to weave into each day's curricular activities in an institutional setting. And yet, in the absence of such faith and practice, there can be no conflict resolution. For without His Spirit, we have, at best, impurity, strife, jealousy, and envy; and, at worst, we have drug addiction, violence, and every other evil thing.

> For the whole Law is fulfilled in one word, in the statement, "You shall love your neighbor as yourself." But if you bite and devour one another, take care lest you be consumed by one another. (Gal. 5:14,15)

Our children need to be in a setting in which virtuous people are in authority—truly in authority. Teachers who are present, but who are not tuned in or prepared to intervene, are not in authority all of the time. For many of us, home is the setting we believe to be ideal. Children can best learn to resolve conflict and become socially competent living and working in close association with those who walk by the Spirit. "Leave the presence of a fool, Or you will not discern the words of knowledge" (Prov. 14:7).

Parents and children living and working together at home have countless opportunities each day to learn and test biblical solutions for human conflict. The Word of God does not tell us to leave our children in the presence of those who lack virtue in order that our children may win them to Christ. The Word tells us the very opposite. We are to be certain that our children are not left in the presence of "a fool." We as parents must discern who and what is foolish. Children, like adults, learn to walk by the Spirit by hearing His Word with faith (Gal. 3:2). Children who live and work with those who walk by the Spirit have the greatest opportunity to learn how to live according to biblical principles.

But what happens when we fail, and the fruit of the Spirit is not present in our lives? If we choose to seek His face, go to His Word, confess our faults, repent, and live in His promises, our hearts will be filled with faith, hope, forgiveness, thanksgiving, and love. When our hearts are filled with faith, hope, forgiveness, thanksgiving, and love, we are able to touch our children's lives with the power of His Word even while our own lives are still under reconstruction.

Faith, Hope, Forgiveness, Thanksgiving, and Love

If our children do not learn to walk in these virtues, then all other pursuits are worth nothing. This is the real business of our lives. Those of us who came to know the Lord in our twenties, thirties, forties, fifties, or anytime later, know that by the power of the Resurrection we can come to know Christ regardless of our training during childhood and adolescence. Even though it is our responsibility as parents to seek His perfect will as we train our children, how reassuring to know that our children are His children first of all. And, He will indeed rescue children who are in the worst possible situations. His grace and mercy will overcome every obstacle.

> For He says to Moses, "I will have mercy on whom
> I have mercy, and I will have compassion on whom
> I have compassion." So then it does not depend on
> the man who wills or the man who runs, but on
> God who has mercy. (Rom. 9:15, 16)

Winning the Lost

Children who are carefully taught from the time they are born are often spared the sorrow of misspent years. But, the body of Christ is diverse; the Lord saves people at every stage of development. Servants of God come from the heart of God according to His perfect will. Throughout Scripture and in all of Church history, God has transformed murderers, cowards, liars, and thieves and equipped them for His ministry. His amazing grace continues forever. Parents teach children to be fit companions for those who are lost by teaching them through the Word that God saves and sanctifies those who are lost no matter how vile and wretched their condition. Children who are fit companions in God's eyes are those who have compassion for the lost and who seek to win them to Christ. This is one of God's standards for social competency. "The fruit of the righteous is a tree of life, And he who is wise wins souls" (Prov. 11:30).

Biblical Role Modeling

In most homeschooling families, the mother is the one who is at home most of the time. Dad is earning a living outside the home. Some mothers and/or fathers have home-based offices, others have home-based businesses. But, in the majority of homeschooling families, the dad goes off to earn a living for some part of every day. We rejoice in the fact—as we consider the lives of the many, many homeschooling families we know—that most of the fathers involve themselves in the daily routine of their households. Even though those fathers are not present for much of the day, they remain tuned-in to what is happening at home. The reason is simple: when the focus of a man's life is the Lord and not his job, his recreational pursuits, or his hobbies, he is free in Christ to become the protector, provider, friend, companion, and servant. Such a dad/husband is an exciting person to know and to receive back into the home each day.

Listening

We must learn to listen if we are to care for one another properly. Listening is a critical part of every relationship. We cannot grow closer to the Lord without learning to listen to Him through His Word; He tells us how to listen to one another. He consoles us when the people we depend upon fail to listen to us. He listens when we speak, and He hears the cry of our hearts when we do not speak. Learning to be socially competent by developing meaningful interpersonal relationships which glorify God, depends on our ability to listen to the Lord and to those around us. Fathers must be listeners.

Life Skills

Most of the homeschooling fathers we know who work outside the home do not come home at night and collapse. Instead, they walk in the door and begin to participate in the lifeflow of the home. And, it is through this flow of life that we learn to become doers of the Word and "not merely hearers who delude themselves" (James 1:22). Home is the place where we best learn the essentials. Fathers, if they are to participate fully in the life of the house, must take part in doing whatever it takes to hold things together. There is much to do in any household that is alive. Some homes are like museums or way stations. But, homes which are shelters and nurturing places are filled with life and activity. Preparing food; cleaning the house; organizing material possessions; washing, drying, folding, and putting away the laundry; bathing, grooming, dressing; maintaining the house, car, lawn, equipment, and everything else we own are all life-skills. Children acquire life-skills by working with their parents and by watching their parents work. This is a great benefit of homeschooling.

If parents are lacking in these skills, they can learn— by His power. When I married Gary, I had the position of associate professor of speech and drama at East Texas Baptist College. I coached a drama team; I was always on the go; I didn't cook, and I hired a maid to clean my small house. The Lord made it clear to me that I needed to change my ways, many, many of my ways. But, I did not realize at thirty-one how very hard it would be. Learning essential life-skills takes a great deal of time if we have not learned to value them. And, in the present culture, essential skills are de-valued. We only learn their value by His Spirit. Learning to serve requires that we have essential skills; serving requires both skill and humility. As we perform the essentials, we learn to serve one another. The Word of God transforms our lives and makes us fit for service. What a privilege it is to live and work with our children; what a privilege to serve them and to witness their delight in serving us and others outside the home. This great business of life, an essential part of social competency, is not learned in the school yard or in the classroom; it is an integral part of life in the home. This reasonable attention to the ordering of our lives is a blessing which home educators can fully enjoy. We pay a price for the privilege of enjoying that blessing, but the worth of it cannot be measured. As we remind ourselves of His purposes, we find meaning in the tasks at hand.

It is not God's will that we "job out" all of the menial tasks in our lives—even when it is in our power to do so. Often, the greatest gift we can offer is the work of our hands. Christ speaks of the essential business of our lives in Matthew 20:25–28:

> You know that the rulers of the Gentiles lord it over them, and their great men exercise authority over them. It is not so among you, but whoever wishes to become great among you shall be your servant, and whoever wishes to be first among you shall be your slave; just as the Son of Man did not come to be served, but to serve, and to give His life a ransom for many.

The most socially competent Christians according to Matthew 20:25–28 are those who have learned to serve. Fathers who work outside the home lead and encourage their families by their willingness to serve them in the home as well.

We Find Biblical Role Models through Age-Integrated Activities

At home in the company of both children and adult friends, in service to people in the community, interacting with adults and other children during projects and productions, children learn to be socially competent through age-integrated activities. First, simply by accompanying their parents, then by serving and working with them, children have the greatest opportunity to become fit companions, bringing honor and glory to God. Chil-

dren and young adults benefit by seeing their parents
interact with a variety of individuals. As the family min-
isters together in the community, children learn to meet
the needs of others and to share the gospel. By working
with adults at church and in the community who love to
serve, children gain wisdom. Children quickly learn to be
kind, gentle, and merciful if they are in the presence of
parents and other adults who have those qualities. Children learn best from those they love and trust; no one
can replace the role of the parents. But, parents must
constantly seek to widen the child's world of mature adult
friendships. Through these friendships, children come to
understand and appreciate God's special dealings in the
lives of His people.

As parents, we need to seek every opportunity to allow our children to witness the struggles, disappointments
and challenges we face in our daily lives. And, as the
Spirit leads us, we need to help our children become
more sensitive to the difficulties which other adults face
as well. As they realize that tribulation is normal and that
His love and protection are certain, they will be prepared
to face the challenges in their own lives. We must answer
their questions and frustrations when adult Christians do
not demonstrate trust in God; and children need to see
that we are eager to encourage those who are weak in the
faith and that we are always ready to rejoice with those
who are strong.

In the world and in the Church, financial pressures,
degenerative disease, and divorce ruin countless lives.
Children need to work through these issues in the course
of growing up in a family. Children benefit by knowing
why their parents make certain financial decisions. If our
goal is to teach our children the value in living debt-free,
they will benefit by knowing how we gain the motivation
and the strength to practice self-denial. Many parents do
not consider it appropriate to discuss their spending hab-
its with their children. Even today, in the Christian community, some parents do not understand the value in

sharing this essential business of life. And, what about choices in food? When parents teach children the connection between diet and disease, and when they demonstrate the joy in planning and preparing and eating whole foods, children are more likely to become wise consumers. When parents and children routinely enjoy physical activities together, children are likely to develop a lifelong desire to remain physically fit.

And, what can they learn about marriage from our marriages? Very little unless we are willing to confess our faults, turn from our sins daily, trust in Christ, and open our lives to our children and to our brothers and sisters in Christ. Transparency makes us accountable, and accountability causes us to look to Christ, knowing that we are truly incapable of walking in victory without Him. To be socially competent in Christ, we must live transparently before our children and before God's people.

> Remind them to be subject to rulers, to authorities, to be obedient, to be ready for every good deed, to malign no one, to be uncontentious, gentle, showing every consideration for all men. For we also once were foolish ourselves, disobedient, deceived, enslaved to various lusts and pleasures, spending our life in malice and envy, hateful, hating one another. But when the kindness of God our Savior and His love for mankind appeared, He saved us, not on the basis of deeds which we have done in righteousness, but according to His mercy, by the washing of regeneration and renewing by the Holy Spirit, who He poured out upon us richly through Jesus Christ our Savior, that being justified by His grace we might be made heirs according to the hope of eternal life.
>
> This is a trustworthy statement; and concerning these things I want you to speak confidently, so that those who have believed God may be careful to engage in good deeds. These things are good and profitable for men. (Titus 3:1–8)

If our children do not understand that as Christians we are accepted in Christ, that our identity is in Him— safe and secure—then our children will suffer greatly. Whenever children compete with one another on the basis of outward beauty, mental ability, athletic ability, and any number of other gifts, talents and skills; whenever they fail to affirm one another in Christ, their relationships become destructive. Children who pronounce other children as unattractive, clumsy, or stupid inflict great pain; and the children who feel worthless as a result of these judgments fail to understand their identity in Christ. Children who are accepted by other children because they are bright and beautiful, often learn to trust in the values of their companions. If children are accepted or rejected on the basis of ungodly standards such as these, then they become victims of a negative, self-centered sociability. If children do not experience a great many age-integrated activities, and if they do not learn the truth of God's Word from Christian adults who are walking by the Spirit, they will be easily deceived. As we mentioned earlier in this chapter, if children remain in the presence of fools, they will not discern the words of knowledge (Prov. 14:7).

As we listen to the concerns of those who teach children ages five and six in public and private schools, we realize that many, many children are surrounded by evil from birth until they are, by His grace, both able and determined to flee from it. Increasing numbers of small children in our society watch the most vile, wicked and violent acts, daily on television. Cable companies, satellite networks, and video stores peddle destruction while helpless children are corrupted. Then, the pitiful children who have been violated and assaulted become the corrupters of those children who are left in their company. Many parents are choosing to rescue their own children while seeking ways to rescue those children who are lost and perishing.

When people ask us, What about socialization? we can best answer if we understand what the inquirer means by the word *socialization*. Then, we can communicate according to God's Word the very essence of what it is to become socially competent in Christ. The opportunities which our children have to interact with other children in homeschool support groups, play groups, church groups, and through community service and numerous other activities are important; however, those activities in and of themselves will not make our children socially competent. Only as we disciple them in Christ and allow them to benefit from biblical role modeling, will their lives exemplify positive, principled sociability.

> For the grace of God has appeared, bringing salvation to all men, instructing us to deny ungodliness and worldly desires and to live sensibly, righteously and godly in the present age, looking for the blessed hope and the appearing of the glory of our great God and Savior, Christ Jesus; who gave Himself for us, that He might redeem us from every lawless deed and purify for Himself a people for His own possession, zealous for good deeds.

> These things speak and exhort and reprove with all authority. Let no one disregard you. (Titus 2:11–15)

Chapter Six

Choosing the Right Curriculum

To put an end to the spirit of inquiry that has characterized the West it is not necessary to burn the books. All we have to do is to leave them unread for a few generations.[1]

I have suggested that the kind of education that will develop the requisite intelligence for democratic citizenship is liberal education, education through great books and the liberal arts, a kind of education that has all but disappeared from the schools, colleges, and universities of the United States.[2]

I attribute this phenomenon to two factors, internal decay and external confusion.[3]

—Robert Maynard Hutchins

It is impossible to have a meaningful discussion about curricula without discussing the value of ideas, ideas which are the very essence of Western civilization. The American Founding Fathers counted "great books" as the chief means of education. They built on the very best of Western thought by studying and discussing those works which had stood the test of time. The tradition of studying great books has been discarded by most educators. There are now many voices, advocating a variety of new methods and materials, who call for multiculturalism and politically correct behavior as the enlightened and compassionate approach. Many Christians whether educated in public schools, private schools, or home schools, with advanced degrees or without them, do not understand the meaning of the great conversation. Without understanding the role of great books in the history of Western civilization and the impact of great books on church and state leaders, we cannot grasp the horror of multiculturalism and political correctness. Multiculturalism is not a search for the objective truth regarding other cultures; rather, it is a denial of objective truth:

> For example, the current popular rejection of "Eurocentrism" and the elevation of "Afrocentrism" in ancient historical studies is not just a difference of opinion over which continent was the more important. The "Afrocentrists" are not just rejecting Europe and western civilization; they and their feminist/gay/socialist allies are attacking historical objectivity itself.[4]

We must understand the value of Western tradition in order to defend it. Robert Hutchins' remarks in volume one of *Great Books of the Western World*, published in 1952, offer us a relevant and insightful answer to the noisy mob that is demanding that our nation abandon the liberal arts and the Judeo-Christian ethic.

> There is no reason why the West should feel that it must apologize for a determination to retain and renew a sense of its own character and its own range. Western civilization is one of the greatest civilizations to date. Not in a spirit of arrogance, but in a spirit of concern that nothing good be lost for the future, the West should take to its meetings with the East a full and vivid sense of its own achievements. Nothing in the main line of the Western tradition leads to ethnocentric pride or cultural provincialism. . . .[5]

> The more dogmatic of those who feel that most of the Western tradition is obsolete, and who take scientific humanism as the new religion, are not

likely to regard the problem of relations with the East as one of understanding, though they will use the phrase.[6]

Primary sources allow us to understand objective truth. The multiculturists are at war with truth. Their agenda is to rewrite history, omit facts, and deny the significance of real people and real events.

A Place to Begin

Books abound which describe the various methods and materials available to home educators. Numerous Christian publishers produce curricula of the highest standards which, of course, reflect their philosophies of education. Many home-educating parents write self-help books, handbooks, and resource guides, and annotate resource catalogues. The individuals and families who pour their very lives into these books, catalogues, and resource guides open windows for all of us who are home educators; and, through these windows, we can survey the ways and means of life in the rich and diversified world of home education. Most home educators, whether novices or veterans, run to these windows often for ideas and encouragement. Some books focus on methods and materials, while others emphasize the significance in first considering various educational philosophies before choosing particular methods and materials. But, we believe that we must begin by understanding our own beliefs.

Zan and I advise and encourage home educators, or prospective home educators, on a regular basis—at separate times and in different places. But, we find that the people we meet have very similar struggles. Many parents who are beginning to homeschool feel as though they are facing an overwhelming research project, that they cannot be effective teachers until they have a thorough understanding of the methods and materials which are available. Some wonder how they will ever learn enough even to begin homeschooling; others can't imagine how they will find the time to prepare for all of the subjects which they need to teach. Veteran homeschoolers often become discouraged: they find that homeschooling is no longer a joy and a blessing; they find the work overwhelming and their lives oppressive. Why does home education become an unbearable burden for many who are capable, diligent, and earnest? Why are Zan and I so certain that anyone can homeschool? Why do we believe that parents who desire to teach their children at home, by the grace of God, will be blessed? And, why do we believe that each of us can discover quite easily what methods and materials will work best for our families?

The answers come to each of us after we have learned to make the proper provision for the journey—and, educating our children at home is indeed a journey. Knowing what provisions are essential for survival determines our success. Parents prepare for homeschooling in a variety of ways; but, in spite of elaborate preparations, some meet with defeat. Many of us do not come to grips with our lack of preparedness until we come up against insurmountable difficulties. And, we all respond differently to the obstacles that we encounter. Some of us, in our beginnings as home educators, realized that we weren't prepared; that we had misunderstood the very nature of the journey; but, like good soldiers, we purposed to learn how to finish the course. We ran, walked, or crawled back to the starting point, discovered what were in fact essential provisions; and set out again. And, by His grace, we purposed to grasp the essentials and found success. The Lord Himself tells us what the essentials are, and by attending to them we are assured of victory in Him.

Others decide to homeschool their children and soon discover that it isn't as they had imagined. The path is foreign to them, and they do not want to travel an unfamiliar road. They do not wish to consider how they might prepare for the journey differently or to acknowledge the great benefits they would derive from the journey. For them, the journey becomes hopeless. They desire only to choose a path they perceive to be more comprehensible and appealing.

Other parents begin the journey with enormous burdens on their backs. They carry supplies they do not need, and they need supplies they do not have. They believe that it is their duty to continue this laborious trek even though their hopes and dreams have not been fulfilled. They miss the blessing of teaching their children because they will not eliminate the distractions. They cannot delight in the tasks at hand because they are consumed by the unnecessaries which they are determined to lug about. They cannot manage the journey because the provisions which they have made are inappropriate. And, consequently, their very lives become unmanageable. They lose their joy.

Preparation for Choosing Methods and Materials

Although each home-educating family makes a journey as unique and multifaceted as the personalities and spiritual gifts of each family member, we all need to focus our time, attention, and energy on the essentials before heading off on our journey. On the outset of our journey, we cannot afford to concern ourselves with the methods, materials, and educational philosophies of others. Although most people who are considering home education believe that the first tasks at hand are to attend curriculum fairs, read curriculum manuals, catalogues, and resource guides, and examine textbooks and educational materials, these tasks are actually distracting, and indeed overwhelming, until we settle the most important issues of parenting. Our essential business is to answer the vital questions: what should I teach my children? and why?

Although it is beyond the scope of this chapter to discuss the many ways in which parents may answer those questions, we can suggest the ways in which various answers lead to certain conclusions regarding instructional methods and materials. I will discuss, in some detail, the way in which our family, and other like-minded educators, have answered these questions. We are not suggesting that our answers have lead us to choose a best way, but rather, the conclusions that we have reached as a result of our answers have lead us to choose what we believe to be the best way for our family. Thoughtful parents go through this process in many different ways; my husband and I have veered off our path now and again as we have tested the choices of others. Again, just because we tested the choices of others and found that their choices didn't meet our needs does not mean that we have concluded that their choices are inferior to our own. Their choices simply didn't work for us. We have attempted to choose instructional methods and materials which are consistent with the way in which we believe He has called us to live.

Recognizing the Diversity in the Body of Christ

Those of us who believe in the inerrancy of Scripture respond to scriptural principles in many different ways. By the power of His Spirit, he leads us to make a variety of choices. As home educators we grow as we embrace others in the body of Christ whose convictions are not our own. We are enlarged by those with whom we differ, just as we are encouraged by those who readily understand our thoughts and feelings about important matters. However, all of us must learn to stand in Him, even if we stand alone for a time. We must trust in His Word as it touches our hearts. Accepting differences in others allows us to learn the lessons which God writes in the lives of His people. Where God embraces and allows such differences, according to Romans 14, we must do the same. This is especially important as parents decide whether or not to homeschool, what instructional methods to choose, which home education magazines to read, and whose advice to follow. No single method or set of materials perform His work in our lives, but, rather, His power working in an infinite number of ways accomplishes that which He chooses, according to His perfect will. We must not, by His grace, seek our identity within the home education movement or any other movement. If we are His, we will find our identity only in Him. We cannot borrow convictions and lifestyles from the writers of books and magazine articles. Praise God for the many, many godly home educators whose words in print are a constant source of encouragement. As their words lead us to His word, we are reminded that nothing of value is accomplished, except by the power of His Spirit. The best advice in print will lead the reader to the Word of God, and, according to Galatians 3, we receive the Spirit by hearing with faith.

Attending to the Essential Business of Our Lives

Therefore, on the outset of this journey we need to attend to the great issues of life. Even though some writers suggest that the time of preparation is best spent considering the various educational philosophies and in determining which aspects of each philosophy might be in harmony with our own, these occupations distract us from the business at hand. The essential business of our lives is 1) to ask the vital questions; 2) to seek Him for the answers; and 3) to set major goals. Asking the basic questions and recognizing our deepest convictions, enable us to set life-goals. These are the matters we must settle before making any other decisions. After we accomplish that, our philosophy of education becomes clear. Answering the vital questions, What should we teach our children? and why? defines our lives as parents. And, while there is no single answer for everyone, all of us need to remain true to the answers which we have found in Christ. After we answer those vital questions, we are ready to make decisions regarding schooling, instructional methods and materials and our personal lifestyles. Those answers will enable us to establish our specific goals. Asking vital questions, finding the answers and establishing our goals is the essential business of our lives.

In preparation for this project, Zan and I surveyed the literature published by and for home educators. I found the task somewhat daunting. The variety of instructional methods and materials and educational resources assures us that the means exists by which we can lighten our load and enrich our lives. However, there are many, many more methods, materials, and resources than any one of us can use in a lifetime. I continue to find relief, and clarity, in returning to the vital questions.

Each of us can know what He would have us to do. Each of us can inspire and be inspired; encourage and be encouraged; advise and be advised—as He leads. But, we cannot know the way in which He will enlarge the very paths beneath the feet of our brothers and sisters (Ps. 31:8). Some readers may answer vital questions in the same way that my husband and I have, and, yet, their course of action may be vastly different. The value lies in sharing our beliefs with one another and in explaining the goals which we have decided are consistent with our beliefs. Answering vital questions, setting goals, and planning a course of action are the essential steps in preparing for our journey. We can profit by sharing that process with one another. Then, after we have worked through the essentials, we are ready for curriculum fairs, curriculum guides, and resource catalogues; they become refreshments along the way. It is a blessing that an abundance of resources are readily available. With our goals clearly in view, choosing methods and materials is a delight. And certainly, success does not depend upon an abundance of financial resources. Financial limitations, like other limitations, cause us to seek Him for specific answers. God uses all of our limitations to direct our steps. We are safe in Him.

Preparing for the Journey

The Essential Questions: What Should We Teach Our Children? And Why?

Our First Answer:

We want our children to know God and to know the ideas which spring from the heart of God. We want our children to know Jesus Christ and to depend upon Him. We want them to know, by the power of His blood, the lovingkindness of our heavenly Father; the identity which is theirs in Christ, our Savior and Advocate; and the comfort and power which is theirs in the Holy Spirit. We want them to understand His Word and to understand biblical principles so thoroughly that by the Spirit they will discern what is of God and what is of the flesh and the devil. We want them to continue learning for all of their lives to think God's thoughts by the Spirit.

And why?

> For to us God revealed them through the Spirit; for the spirit searches all things, even the depths of God. For who among men knows the thoughts of a man except the spirit of the man, which is in him? Even so the thoughts of God no one knows except the Spirit of God. Now we have received, not the spirit of the world, but the Spirit who is from God, that we might know the things freely given to us by God, which things we also speak, not in words taught by human wisdom, but in those taught by the Spirit, combining spiritual thoughts with spiritual words.

> But a natural man does not accept the things of the Spirit of God; for they are foolishness to him, and he cannot understand them, because they are spiritually appraised. But he who is spiritual appraises all things, yet he himself is appraised by no man. FOR WHO HAS KNOWN THE MIND OF THE LORD, THAT HE SHOULD INSTRUCT HIM? But we have the mind of Christ. (1 Cor. 2:10–16)

Our Second Answer:

We want our children to know the great thinkers (as the world counts great) and the great Christians (as God's people have counted as great) and to consider the ideas and the deeds by which they are known. We want our children to understand what is meant by the great conversation, the words which have endured for centuries because men through time have considered them the finest creations, in writing, of the Western mind. The tradition of the West is embodied in the great conversation that began in the dawn of history and that continues to the present day. We stand with those who are "convinced that the West needs to recapture and re-emphasize and bring to bear upon its present problems the wisdom that lies in the works of its greatest thinkers"[7] if we are to remain civilized. We want our children to know that these books are intelligible to the them, and that no teacher or textbook writer ought to come between them and the authors. We want them to know that while we are glad to discuss each author's work, it remains the business of their lives to consider which authors are right and which authors are wrong according to the Word of God. By tuning into this great conversation that has gone on for twenty-five centuries, we trust that our children will discern by the Spirit the great errors and the great truths as they have been expressed by the greatest writers in the history of Western civilization.

We want our children to understand the quality of thinking expressed by the American Founding Fathers by reading their letters, diaries, and state papers. We want them to consider the standard by which early Americans judged our Founding Fathers to be educated; and by doing so, to comprehend the present state of decay in American education.

We want our children to know the men and women who have changed the world for Christ. We want them to hear directly from those saints whose written works have been preserved in order that they may understand and value these lives that have lead others to triumph in Christ.

We want our children to learn to enjoy many of the books which are considered classics and to spend pleasant hours delighting in books which are simply good. We want our children to enjoy those living books which will help them to grow emotionally, spiritually, and intellectually sound.

And why? We believe that by learning which ideas have shaped Western civilization and by considering the thoughts and deeds of those who have changed the world for the sake of the gospel, we enrich our lives and the lives of others. We believe that as we focus on the great ideas and deeds, the places and dates and events surrounding those ideas and deeds acquire meaning. The chronology of ideas and deeds brings to life that which we consider a liberal arts education. We learn the connection between earlier works and later ones as we study ideas. The early works contribute to the development of later writers, and later writers do us the favor of interpreting earlier works.

"The Medium Is the Message"[8]

The medium of print allows us to interact with the ideas; we are active participants in the conversation. We grow as we read good books and great books. The electronic media makes us passive; we can endure very little of it without becoming weakened by it. If we are to inspire a generation which can change the world, we must teach that generation to read, write, speak, and listen. Children must learn to love that which is good, and children must love to learn.

After answering the vital questions, we are able to clarify our goals, prioritize our activities, and choose our educational methods and materials.

The Major Goals for Our Family

1. Lead the family in personal devotions, family devotions and family worship, and Bible study in order that by His Spirit these activities will have preeminence in our lives.

2. Read the good books and the great books aloud to our children, acknowledging that by doing this we will greatly improve the quality of each of our lives.

3. Use textbooks, reference books and a variety of educational resources as tools which assist us in organizing the great ideas and which inspire us to consider and reconsider them; but never use textbooks or other educational materials as substitutions for the original, unabridged writings of the authors themselves.

4. Organize time and material possessions in ways that allow each of the disciplines of life—liberal arts, fine arts, computational skills, communications skills, and life-skills—to impact our growth and development.

5. Live with our children as fellow-learners.

Understanding the Educational Philosophies Out of Which Methods and Materials Have Grown

As Christians I think we do well to become eclectic in regard to assumptions about life and learning. By the Spirit we are able to understand which ideas are consistent with biblical principles and which ideas are not. We are also able to understand the areas in which we have great liberty. I found one author's description of four educational philosophies to be especially interesting (Mary Hood, Ph.D., *Countdown to Consistency, A Workbook for Home Educators*. [Westminster, Maryland: n.p., 1992]). Although some people may fall in one particular category or another, the author believes (and I agree) that it is unlikely that many will find one system of thought which fits them perfectly. Dr. Hood is an educational consultant and homeschooling mother whose dissertation (1990) is entitled *Contemporary Philosophical Influences on the Home-Schooling Movement*. Her small booklet on the subject would be useful to anyone, novice or veteran home educator.[9] I will use Dr. Hood's four categories and briefly discuss the ideas we have accepted, and those we have rejected, from each system. Zan and I believe that the freedom in eclecticism reflects our liberty in the Lord.

Zan and I talk to many home educators who have grown weary and disheartened because they have patterned their lives after a certain speaker or author. Or, they feel compelled to embrace the lifestyle promoted by a certain leader in the home education movement, even though the leader's convictions and opinions are not their own. Any Christian can fall into this trap if their need for acceptance is not met in Christ. We all need affirmation and desire it, but we must come to the revelation that our acceptance and our identity is in Christ—if we are to be safe and free in Him. Often, homeschooling families fail to find support in the local church; then, perhaps, their neighbors and family members, who are unbelievers, are unsupportive as well. Consequently, they seek their identity through someone, or some group, within the home education movement. But, it is by His Spirit that we find comfort, guidance, and security. My husband and I are comfortable with the choices we have made and certain about the beliefs which we hold regarding the education of our children. But, we are not at all certain that anyone can or should make the same choices we've made. Every home educating family must have the liberty to determine what methods and materials are most useful for them. After we answer the vital questions and establish our educational goals, we need never be distracted or confused by the choices of others. His Spirit directs our paths.

Eclecticism

> **eclectic** adj. 1. Choosing what appears to be the best from diverse sources, systems or styles consisting of that which has been selected from diverse sources. -n. One who follows an eclectic method.[10]

I will comment briefly upon the significance of several philosophies of education and then discuss the methods and materials which best characterize each philosophy of education. By expressing why I believe that I have gleaned the best from each educational philosophy, I hope to encourage readers to exercise that same freedom as they choose methods and materials which are consistent with their beliefs and goals. The choices we have made will be inappropriate for those who have goals which are different from ours; our choices will also be inappropriate for anyone whose thoughts, feelings, and convictions differ from ours. Each of us needs to know where the Spirit is leading and to trust in Him.

Essentialism

In our opinion, the best thoughts that characterize this educational philosophy are 1) the conviction that objective truth and absolute values are the basis for all knowledge, and 2) the view that there is an essential body of knowledge that ought to be transmitted to the next generation. Essentialists who are also Christians trust in the authority of God's Word and discern truth and error by faith in the Word. However, I do not share the views of most essentialists in regard to curriculum choices, lesson planning, methods of instructing, and evaluating our children. Many essentialists literally bring the schoolhouse to the home. Flags, posters, bulletin boards, special days, school colors, ridged schedules, workbooks, worksheets, textbooks, quizzes, multiple choice examinations, school desks, completely scheduled days, lessons planned in advance, adherence to teacher guides, characterize the essentialist's homeschool experience.

Essentialists tend to advocate a curriculum which is subject-centered. They use textbooks for English literature, history, geography, etc. Children focus on the subjects that they are taking. Most of the elementary schools, secondary schools, and undergraduate schools use textbooks as the primary educational resource for every subject. In contrast to this, anyone pursuing a doctor of philosophy degree, or many other advanced degrees, relies on primary sources.

Many of us believe that the time to begin focusing on primary sources and worthy books is during early childhood. Children learn the language they hear; and quality counts. William Bennett's inspiring anthology, *The Book of Virtues*, is an excellent example of worthy writings which benefit very small children. Audio tapes are available for parents who do not feel that they are prepared to perform literature. My husband and I, like many of our friends, read aloud to each other as well as to the children. All of us improve by listening to the very best thoughts. Textbooks, for many of us, have a different role; like reference books, scope and sequence charts, and numbers of other educational resources, they are tools. At our home, we use a number of Bob Jones textbooks, but we no longer purchase the teacher's guides. I am not a classroom teacher; and, as I have explained, our learning is not subject-centered. We discuss the ideas of various people, as well as the places and events surrounding their lives; the older children read to the younger children, and I read to each of the children individually. My husband and I read to the children or family as a group. The older girls read silently as well. When the two younger children need my direct instruction, the older children use textbooks, work texts, and a variety of reference books for information and instruction. They enjoy using well-written, attractive textbooks from time to time. But, the textbooks are tools for enrichment. The focus of our studies is people, what they think, what they've done, and how they have expressed themselves. By reading aloud to our children from the time that they are small, we allow them to connect with the authors, with the other members of the family; we share the very best of life together. Surely, the Word of God needs to be experienced by families in this way.

If reading aloud continues forever, and silent reading begins as soon as the children are able to read independently, then blocks of time are required. Parents who choose to do this and who see the value in it, soon discover how very much curricula they do not need. They have time to read because they do not have to concern themselves with crowd control. Bells and lesson plans do not limit discussion. Breakfast, lunch, and dinner are as meaningful as all of the other learning times in between.

Good biographies and autobiographies fascinate children and adults. People's lives and thoughts stimulate our interest in geography, history, and language. Learning is interdisciplinary. Children ought to have free access to numerous textbooks and anthologies. Knowing how editors and publishers include, omit, edit, and organize information is an important part of each child's education. Those choices reflect our culture—both the anti-Judeo-Christian culture and the Judeo-Christian tradition. Children need to realize that educators have different ideas about what is worth knowing. As we give children access to a variety of instructional materials, and as we describe to them various methods of instruction, we are imparting valuable knowledge about our culture. Attending curriculum fairs and reading curriculum handbooks, resource catalogues, and manuals enables children to understand the diversity in the body of Christ and the necessity in setting goals for themselves.

During the upper elementary grades, students need to be well acquainted with some of the controversies concerning the contents of the textbooks which are used in both public and private schools. As our children begin to understand the struggles within our culture, they grow more sensitive to the problems of those who have been indoctrinated by the world. The home environment, the close relationship between parents and their children, and the direction of the Holy Spirit allow home educators to bless their children with a variety of methods and materials which might not be appropriate in a conventional classroom setting.

While many of us share the essentialist's view that a particular body of knowledge exists which must be transmitted to the next generation, we do not advocate the subject-centered way in which the body of knowledge is often taught. I am particularly fond of the well-known *Core Knowledge Series* by E. D. Hirsch. Although this series is rejected by home educators who believe that there is no essential body of knowledge which ought to be transmitted to the next generation; many of us who believe that there are essentials find this series provides excellent guidelines for transmitting those essentials. I believe that the series is a delightful and useful resource. Home educators who oppose this view of an essential body of knowledge contend that the ordering of such knowledge (for grades one through six) is absurd and that the purpose of such works is to satisfy the need which institutions have for organizational control and order. However, without essential knowledge our children cannot understand our country's background in Western civilization as well as other areas and cultures. Children can read the Hirsch series alone or with a parent in order to acquire an understanding of the scope and sequence of essential knowledge; then the ideas, people, and places in the living books come to life within a historical context. The *Core Knowledge Series* helps both the parents and children to grasp the big picture and to acquire an adequate background knowledge of mainstream culture. The books don't require lesson plans; parents and children simply need to read them.

Many essentialists use numerous textbooks to provide a core curriculum; those of us who focus on primary resources, but who have many essentialist tendencies, appreciate E. D. Hirsch's series. Home educators who rely on the standard textbook approach to core curriculum (e.g., A Beka textbooks and Bob Jones textbooks) generally feel compelled to follow the teacher guides and to teach the subjects as the publishers advise. This is extremely time-consuming and makes it nearly impossible for the parents and the children to spend hours reading real books. Through the Hirsch series, we can move quite breezily back into the primary sources. However, many families prosper by using the core curricula provided by major Christian publishers. The textbooks and teacher's guides offer the support and guidance that some home educators require. Linear texts offer a time-proven method of instruction; the excerpts of various author's works, as well as the unabridged versions of some works, offer all that many parents desire. For some parents a focus on living books and primary sources is far too time-consuming for students in elementary and secondary school.

Other home educators with whom I am acquainted found the task of educating their children at home—by using textbooks and teacher's guides—to be so burdensome that they felt compelled to put their children back into school. They are aware of other instructional methods and materials, but they understand this system of learning best; it is what they encountered in school. They reason that if they don't have the time and energy to cover all of the subjects, as the textbooks and the teacher's guides require, they need to send their children to a classroom teacher who can.

Essentialists also tend to evaluate learning through objective tests, emphasizing the importance of remembering factual material. Many of us believe that oral and written discussions of important ideas and information are more meaningful. Our children discuss what they are reading and thinking with each other and with my husband or me at various times throughout the day. They know that it is important to remember a great many things. From time to time they initiate the practice of taking tests at the ends of the chapters in textbooks they happen to be reading. They find it at least as interesting as working crossword puzzles. They realize that it is important to know the facts. They also learn useful information through music—the younger children sing the names of the presidents of the United States, the United States by region, the capitals, the countries of the world, and on and on. But, the way in which we as parents evaluate what we have learned is by oral or written expression. We have conversations, make speeches, and teach classes; we write letters, articles, or books. Our children need to evaluate what they have learned by the same methods. I don't think multiple choice or true-false tests tells us what children know, and they certainly don't help children learn to communicate what they know.

Perennialism

Perennialists focus on the books and ideas which are timeless, and, like the essentialists, they believe in absolute values and eternal truth. Christians who are perennialists believe that God's Word is truth and that it is the absolute standard for good and evil. Perennialists consider learning a lifelong process and view youth as a preparatory stage. This is consistent with biblical truth. We understand from Proverbs and Titus, to name only two books in the Bible, that we are to learn from those who are older. A man or woman who is godly in his youth and who continues to grow in grace and knowledge will be wiser still when he or she is old. Scripture places great value on the wisdom of older men and women who walk with the Lord.

We believe that children ought to have a sense of what it has meant throughout history to be educated. In the preface of *The Great Conversation, The Substance of a Liberal Education* (1952), author Robert M. Hutchins, expresses the perennialist's view:

> Until lately the West has regarded it as self-evident that the road to education lay through great books. No man was educated unless he was acquainted with the masterpieces of his tradition. There never was very much doubt in anybody's mind about which the masterpieces were. They were the books that had endured and that the common voice of mankind called the finest creations, in writing, of the Western mind.[11]

No one ever gets finished with these works in the sense that we are ever done with them. They enlarge us;

and, then, as we grow, we experience them even more fully. Reading many of these works to our children and young adults certainly is of immeasurable benefit to the entire family.

Perennialists prepare students for self-discipline in a way that the essentialists do not. Perennialists emphasize the importance of the student having direct contact with the author—with no textbook summaries or explanations to get in the way. The goal is for the student to initiate contact with the author and to consider the author's contribution by using his own ability to reason; it becomes the student's responsibility to take part in the great conversation.

The works of English educator Charlotte Mason (1842–1923) have become prominent in the home education movement. She believed that students should read many worthy books in order to become liberally educated. There are many great writers, as well as numbers of very good writers, who are not part of the select group who are included in the great conversation. Charlotte Mason considered all worthy books to be vital to liberal education. Most proponents of liberal education agree with this view. The reason that Robert Hutchins did not include the works of Emerson, Whitman, Thoreau, and Mark Twain in the *Great Works of the Western World* is best explained in his own words:

> We thought it no part of our duty to emphasize national contributions, even those of our own country. I omitted Emerson, Whitman, Thoreau, and Mark Twain, all very great writers, because I felt that, important as they were, they did not measure up to the other books in the set. They carried forward the Great Conversation, but not in such a way as to be indispensable to the comprehension of it. Obviously in a set made up of a limited number of volumes only the writers that seemed indispensable could be included.[12]

Susan Schaeffer Macaulay's book, *For the Children's Sake: Foundations of Education for Home and School* has done much to bring the concept of liberal education in general, and Charlotte Mason's teaching in particular, to the attention of the homeschool community.[13] Many of the proponents of the liberal arts are not Christians, and, as a result, they do not grasp the possibilities of childhood. Charlotte Mason certainly did comprehend the possibilities of childhood. All parents who are walking by the Spirit want their children to know the abundant life; we want them to be dear, teachable, and ready to receive. Ever since Christ began His ministry on earth, many who have named His name have missed the wonder of Life in Him. He offers us the revelation of how we must come to Him:

> Truly I say to you, unless you are converted and become like children, you shall not enter the kingdom of heaven. Whoever then humbles himself as this child, he is the greatest in the kingdom of heaven. And whoever receives one such child in My name receives Me; but whoever causes one of these little ones who believe in Me to stumble, it is better for him that a heavy millstone be hung around his neck, and that he be drowned in the depth of the sea. (Matt. 18:3–6)

No matter how thoughtfully and carefully we introduce living books to our children and no matter how we classify the books (great books, classics, good books, worthy books), they will not enrich and enlighten our children unless we have, by His grace, been able to lead our children to an appreciation of God's Word and a dependence upon Him. Susan Schaeffer Macaulay's Christian world view, her appreciation for the fullness of life in Christ, and her excellent introduction to Charlotte Mason have motivated many of us to read the original works of Charlotte Mason. Christian parents need to examine the fact that what they believe may be part of an even greater conversation, one in which the Lord would surely have them be a part. As Christian liberal artists, we see possibilities that the natural mind cannot dream. We believe that the journals, letters, and writings of Christians throughout history—many of them missionaries and evangelists—are essential works, in our view of liberal education.

Our only caution regarding perennialism, a movement with which we clearly identify, is that an emphasis on the great works must be balanced by a determination to understand His work in the lives of His people, on all continents, through all of recorded history. With an eternal perspective, we are able to look upon the people and events of our lives as precious moments in His hands. We can then understand the ways in which beliefs affect events. The historic Christian faith has shaped—and continues to shape—lives and events in countless ways.

Living Books

I remember that my father read all of Mark Twain's *Tom Sawyer* to me when I was quite young. I was impressed by the large volume with small print and the wonderful words he spoke from it. I also remember how great it was to read *Jane Eyre* in elementary school after my mother introduced me to the Bronte sisters. I have no memory of anything that I read during elementary school hours at that time, but I remember vividly the books mother gave me at home. Surely, it is because I simply met the authors. The first real excitement that I remember from any reading assignment in school came during my high school drama class in tenth grade, consequently I took drama each year until high school graduation. I read Aeschylus, Sophocles, Euripides, Aristophanes, Thornton Wilder, Shakespeare—I connected with worlds and people and ideas far beyond my limited experience and imagination. From then on I made time for living books.

In undergraduate school, through the compassion of good teachers, I found writers whose plays and poetry and essays opened the only windows that I knew existed, the windows of the mind. I did not know Christ, but I longed to find meaning and beauty in life.

Then, two years after I had become a Christian and the same month that I finished my masters degree, I began preparing for a doctor of philosophy degree in the Department of Speech at Louisiana State University. I found myself under the tutelage of liberally educated people. I decided then, and have grown more certain in the seventeen years since then, that children ought to be educated in much the same way that my professors, proponents of the liberal arts, taught me at Louisiana State University. They introduced me to people, people with important ideas, through the words which they wrote; nothing came between the authors and speakers and myself—no textbooks, no interpretations. I just read the author's words. I studied under professors, both men and women, of character whose eyes sparkled when they listened to ideas and who always had time to discuss those ideas with me. The tests and hurdles of graduate school were simply the price for admission, and they were well worth it. The spirit of inquiry changed my life. The discipline of this process of education, this working through ideas, is important. It is available to all of us; no degree program is required. This is the education which our children need. And, only the best books, beginning with the Word of God, can give it to them.

I wandered into a bookstore near the LSU campus and found two books by writers I had never heard about; those writers were Francis and Edith Schaeffer. Through their works, I began to understand what it means to live fully as a Christian. *L'Abri* by Edith Schaeffer and *The God Who Is There* by Francis Schaeffer gave me hope that God has a purpose for all of His people in all of their diversity. I traveled to Dallas, Texas, to hear Dr. Schaeffer speak during the promotional tour for his book, *How Should We*

Then Live. During the three years that I prepared for my
doctor of philosophy degree, I had time to read and to
think about what it means to be liberally educated. And,
through the works of Francis Schaeffer, I developed a
Christian world view, a sense of God's work through man
in all of his diversity, throughout all of recorded time. I
held on tightly to the simplicity of the gospel, to the
Word which I heard faithfully preached by my Acadian
French pastor in Lafayette, Louisiana, and to the precious saints that God so mercifully sent into my life. All
of those experiences shaped my ideas concerning the
education of both children and adults. I learned that only
by the Spirit do we recognize what is great in the mind
of God.

Perennialism describes the classical education popular for many years in Europe, a philosophy of education
emphasizing the significance of literature, language, and
history. Certainly, it describes the educational philosophy
of Robert Hutchins and Mortimer Adler, as well; in the
Great Books of the Western World, the editors include epic
and dramatic poetry, satires, and novels. Histories and
works in ethics, economics, politics, and jurisprudence
are represented; and both mathematics and the natural
science—works in astronomy, physics, chemistry, biology,
and psychology—are represented. But, we cannot see Light
or escape the pitch without a knowledge of Him. Charlotte Mason brings the very life of Christ into perennialism
and focuses on the great importance of real life, real
work, real books in the lives of children. In contrast to
Robert Hutchins' view of childhood and youth as a dark
and dreadfully limited time, Charlotte Mason perceived
that a child can be awakened by the Spirit.

Perennialists, having great respect and appreciation
for the great and good books, generally avoid the use of
textbooks. Some educators in this group dismiss textbooks altogether as "twaddle," borrowing Charlotte
Mason's term. Again, we do well to respect the choices of
other people. I think of the countless numbers of children who have led victorious, rich, and interesting lives

in Christ before, during, and after years of reading and studying textbooks. It is arrogant and ignorant to imagine that people who do not use certain methods or materials are destined to miss out on anything we might imagine. God is sovereign, and He will make of our lives what He will. Many godly parents, committed to Christ, use full service textbook suppliers, and many rely on teacher's manuals for the guidance they are seeking. Others find success with curriculum providers. The educational objectives of Christian educators are not the same; therefore, they will not choose the same methods and materials. Just as the use of textbooks and curriculum packages is confining and burdensome to some parents; life without those materials seems incomplete and chaotic to others. We learn what to do by seeking and praying and then trusting in His goodness and mercy.

Dr. Hood's third and fourth categories, progressivism and Existentialism, are interesting. However, it is important to keep in mind that although these two educational philosophies gave birth to methods and materials which are now popular with a number of home educators; many home educators do not share the educational philosophy of the progressives or the existentialists. It is perfectly clear why essentialists and perennialists choose certain methods and materials; specific methods and materials help them to reach their goals. But, the methods and materials which serve the existentialists and the pragmatists also accommodate a variety of educational philosophies and belief systems. Having said that, there is some value in considering the way in which people whose value systems are diametrically opposed to each other choose similar methods and materials.

Progressivism

Progressivism grew out of pragmatism, which is rooted in Darwinian evolutionary theory. The pragmatic philosophers believe that truth is relative. Since they believe that traditions which are based on religion are invalid, they develop concepts of ethics and morality which can be adapted to what they perceive to be "the needs of modern man."

> **pragmatism** n. 1. Philosophy. The Theory, developed by Charles S. Pierce and William James, that the meaning of a proposition or course of action lies in its observable consequences, and that the sum of these consequences constitutes its meaning. 2. A method or tendency in the conduct of political affairs characterized by the rejection of theory and precedent, and by the use of practical means and expedients.[14]

Social reconstructionists view schools as the agents of social change, and their goal is the development of socialism in America. John Dewey and the progressive education movement dominated the 1940s, and many of their ideas remain intact today: progressive slogans which we hear today from both educators in the public school arena and within the home education movement are "whole child," "active learning," "creative self-expression," and "unit instruction."

The goal of progressivism is to encourage children to adapt to a society which is ever evolving. Since progressivists believe that there is no absolute truth (in contrast to the essentialists and the perennialists who believe in the existence of objective truth and absolute values); they conclude that children need to learn to adapt to each situation as it presents itself. Schools are essential for socialization according to this philosophy because children need to learn to adapt to the ethics and morals of an ever-changing society. Progressives view the tasks of planning, instruction, and evaluation as an opportunity for the teachers (parents) and children to work as a team.

In the hands of Christian home educators, the unit study approach is not used to accomplish the sinister goals of social reconstructionism. It would be impossible for me to imagine a more rich and valuable means of teaching biblical truth than from the "Wisdom Booklets," unit studies produced by Bill Gothard's Advanced Training Institute. The Christians who developed this curriculum using the unit study approach, like other Christians using this approach, do not subscribe to the educational philosophies of progressivism or the theory of pragmatism.

Author Valerie Bendt's delightful book *How to Create Your Own Unit Studies* emphasizes the value of living books and offers a treasury of ways in which to use real books and real life. Here are the components of a unit study the author created on World Geography: Art Activities and Creative Writing Assignments; Games and Puzzles; Non-Fiction Books; Fiction Books; Study of Geography Terms and Definitions; Video Cassettes and Audio Cassettes; Bible Verses; Numerous Publications; Field Trips; Memorization Work.[15]

Perennialists can certainly use these methods and materials to achieve their goals. Those of us who believe that there is an essential body of knowledge that we ought to transmit to the next generation (essentialism); and, those of us who believe, as did the American Founding Fathers, that we must study the ideas in the Western tradition in order to understand our own character, and in order to preserve our own good, tend toward a linear approach to education. We see that the earlier ideas prepare us for later ones, and that we better understand the ideas of the seventeenth-century writers if we already have a knowledge of the works which those men read. Those of us who feel most comfortable organizing ideas by using a linear approach use living books and even textbooks to lay a solid foundation; we use unit studies to enrich our lives and enlarge our vision. Christian educators who advocate unit studies do not have the same goals or philosophical base that the progressives or the pragmatists have. They encourage the use of worthy books and real life; they study people and their ideas. A number of publishers sell units prepared in advance (e.g., these include the Konos and Weaver curricula).

Unit studies are a wonderful means by which large
families can work together and enrich each other's lives.
They offer an endless number of possibilities. Many of us
use unit studies to complement a linear approach. For
instance, a good unit study can bring the Scripture to life
if we continue to study the Bible in a linear fashion. The
Bible begins in Genesis and ends in Revelation by design;
there is great value in reading it from beginning to end.
Charlotte Mason advocated narration as a means of evaluating what the students had learned. One of our long-
term goals as a family is for each of us to learn and
narrate the major events, biblical principles, important
passages, and key people in each book of the Bible from
Genesis to Revelation. This family walk through the Bible
seems to us to be dependent upon a linear approach.

Existentialism

> **existentialism** n. A body of ethical thought, cur-
> rent in the 19th. and 20th. centuries, centering
> about the uniqueness and isolation of individual
> experience in a universe indifferent or even hostile
> to man, regarding human existence as unexplain-
> able, and emphasizing man's freedom of choice
> and responsibility for the consequences of his acts.[16]

As an unbeliever in undergraduate school, I found
my identity in the existentialist movement. I read Soren
Kierkegaard, Jean Paul Sartre, Albert Camus, and the
Absurdists. And, while non-Christian home educators may
find their philosophy rooted in this movement, certainly
no child of God does. But, I believe that some of the best
ideas and some of the worst ideas concerning the education of young children are found in the books written by
those who do in fact identify with the existentialists. That
shouldn't surprise us because Satan comes as an angel of
light.

Most existentialist educators do not consider it appropriate to choose the curriculum for the student. They
lead students to place value in being authentic, honest,

and trustworthy; and in forming interpersonal relationships. It is beyond the scope of this chapter to discuss
existentialism in any meaningful way. But, certainly, it is
important for parents and older students to read the
works of the existentialists and to identify those ideas
which are consistent with biblical truth and those concepts which are based on deception and error.

John Holt, the well-known educator who is considered the father of "unschooling," "free" and "invited"
learning, has written what many of us consider to be
classic works in the areas of homeschooling and educational reform. With the Holy Spirit as our guide, John
Holt challenges us to come to terms with our educational
practices and to reexamine the principles on which our
educational goals are based. Those of us who see wisdom
in learning basic skills (the world calls it self-sufficiency)
and in being good stewards of our time and resources
(the world calls it self-reliance) have much in common
with the existentialists in the home education movement.
We see virtue in home-births, alternative medicine, home
churches, home-based businesses, growing our own food.
We see potential in each individual family member and
believe that our potential continues to be realized throughout the entire course of our lives. As parents, we see
ourselves as fellow learners, as facilitators as well as instructors. Many home educators who are truly existentialists see themselves as facilitators only. Many of us with
many of the same tendencies as home educators who are
existentialists find that advance planning is often stifling;
we let the lessons carry us where they will. Because we are
interested in ideas, we value the expressive arts. We rarely
test; we never label; and we encourage ourselves, our
spouse, and our children to develop a variety of skills.

John Holt's books were the first homeschooling books
that I read. I read them during my master's program in
reading. I recommend them to Christians who are rooted
and grounded in God's Word. To those who are not rooted
and grounded in the Word, I recommend nothing except

Colossians 3:6–9. We must make the vital decisions which
effect the lives of our children by the power of the Holy
Spirit. Without the truth of who we are in Christ, we
become captive to the beliefs, attitudes, and values of
others. We cannot walk in another man's convictions; we
must hear from the Lord ourselves. We find ourselves in
bondage when we try to live up to the ideals of others. All
of us need to find our particular path in Christ Jesus—in
Him and Him alone. Many of John Holt's ideas are in-
consistent with the biblical principles, but if we walk by
the Spirit we can learn much from this gentle man who
loved teaching children.

Both the Instructional Setting and the Relationship between the Student and the Teacher Redefine Instructional Methods and Materials and Determine Their Effectiveness

Some readers may be inclined to dismiss the educational methods and materials which have been inspired
by the progressives and existentialists as trendy and destructive because they have contributed to chaos in the
public classrooms. Many of the educators who have made
such judgments have done so on the basis of the results
in both the public and private classrooms; they have witnessed the disintegration of educational achievement.
Institutions are wise to reject the values and goals (and
many methods and materials) of the progressives and the
existentialists. Many of us believe that the enrichment
activities promoted by the progressives and the lifestyle
and human development issues encouraged by the existentialists are the real business of parents. Educators have
unwittingly cultivated aimlessness by failing to identify
the essentials and by failing to focus on the perennial.
Progressives and existentialists compromise the school
day at private and public institutions, by attempting to
restructure the family and society in their own image.
However, home educators, by the Spirit, are able to use

a variety of methods (even those methods which have been popularized by misguided educational theorists—progressives, existentialists, or whomever) to impart wisdom.

In order to provide meaningful examples of the ways in which like-minded people make different choices in methods and materials, I will mention one of the institutions which I admire most, Hillsdale College. If we understand the opportunities and challenges that educators face in the teacher-directed, classroom setting—as opposed to the opportunities and challenges which educators face in the parent-directed homeschool setting—we can better appreciate each other's differences. The fact that home educators use certain methods and materials which have created chaos in public and private classrooms, does not mean those methods will promote chaos in homeschools. Likewise, methods and materials which are sterile and confining in a homeschool may be of practical value in a public or private classroom setting.

U.S. News and World Report and *Barrons* have ranked Hillsdale College among the best small colleges in the country. Never in the college's 150-year history have they accepted federal funds or federal control. The college opened Hillsdale Academy in 1990 as an extension of the college's Teacher Education Program. They have put forth a model for the development of other alternative schools. Their educational philosophy reflects both essentialism and perennialism. They see themselves as allies of the family and seek to reinforce the efforts of the parents "to guide the intellectual, emotional, and spiritual development of their children." Hillsdale Academy offers the *Hillsdale Academy Reference Guide* to interested parents and educators who seek to reform the current educational agenda. Sections included in the guide are: "School Culture," "K-8 Curriculum," "Reading Lists," "Bibliography," "Additional Titles List," "Publishers' List," "Parents' Handbook," and "Faculty Handbook." I believe that this is an excellent resource for parents homeschooling their own children. A letter from George Roche, president of Hillsdale College, is part of the introduction to the guide:

> Hillsdale Academy operates on two basic assumptions: children need to learn and adults need to teach them. On the face of it, that assertion would seem to be common sense. But over the years since the concept of "progressive education" first gained popularity, schools, teachers, and educational theorists have tended to lose sight of this simple truth.[17]

The relationship between the classroom teacher and the student is a formal one, and the time allotted to learning is necessarily limited by the school hours. The instructor must be in a teaching mode all of the time and adhere to a fixed schedule in order to cover the essentials. Home educators, on the other hand, have decided to bring their children home to life, to what many of us believe is the real business of life. And, in this real business, the academic disciplines are only a part of what we believe to be essential. Yes, we are teachers, but most of us consider ourselves fellow-learners because it is by watching our response to new tasks, new information, new experiences, new revelations, that our children truly grow. Because we as parents interact with our children all day, each day, in a casual and cooperative way, we can enjoy a "values-centered curriculum that stresses facts, logical concepts, and intelligent language"[18] (as outlined in the *Hillsdale Academy Reference Guide*). And yet, we can do so without "relying on well-established instructional techniques proven over centuries"[19] (as exemplified by the Hillsdale Academy teachers). We believe that the tutorial method is the oldest and the most reliable way to teach both children and adults. George Roche's letter goes on to say:

> From the quite sensible observation that children are unique individuals with their own special talents and interests, many educators erroneously

conclude that no curriculum can meet all their needs and that education is best when it leaves children at liberty to learn what they want in the ways they like best. The all-too-frequent result of this approach has been educational chaos. That chaos is compounded by increasing demands that teaching styles and subject content be flexible enough to meet the special interests of children from different cultural groups. Such an educational vision puts the student in charge, glorifying individuality, but ultimately depriving children of what they need most: knowledge and adult direction.[20]

Parents teaching their own children simply have a different set of possibilities and challenges than do educators working in even the best private institutions. Many of us have concluded that no curriculum can meet the needs of all our children; however, we do not all believe that our children are then "at liberty to learn what they want in the ways they like best."[21] But, before we comment further on the benefits of drawing from several curricula, I will share my own thoughts regarding learning styles.

Many home educators do feel compelled to discover what their children want to learn and how they will best learn it. They often dismiss ideas such as those which George Roche has expressed as harsh and insensitive and part of the hostile classroom environment. But, many of us who work closely with our children know that learning style theories do not answer every challenge. The world of people with whom they will form relationships, and with whom they must learn to communicate, will not try to figure out how to best reach them or to understand their learning styles. But, rather, the burden will be upon our children to learn to reach outside of themselves and to discover how to touch the world.

Mary Pride's *Big Book of Home Learning, Vol.1* provides an excellent overview of learning style theory. Many of us have little patience with learning style theories based

on Jungian psychology or other psychological theories.
However, we often find it both interesting and helpful to
consider classifications of personality types, learning pat-
terns, and instructional strategies. The most concise, lively,
interesting, and useful book I have read on the subject of
learning styles is *The Way They Learn, How to Discover and
Teach to Your Child's Strengths* written by Cynthia Ulrich
Tobias and published by Focus on the Family.[22] Many of
us believe that while it is essential for both adults and
children to consider how they themselves, and others
around them, learn best; it is a great mistake to focus
entirely on "teaching to the other person's need"—whether
the student is a child or an adult. "Iron sharpens iron, so
one man sharpens another" (Prov. 27:17). As a result of
friction we become a paradox; necessarily sharp and
wonderfully smooth. None of us should be deprived—as
learners—of discovering how to adapt and accommodate.
My husband Gary and I are opposites in the way we
perceive information and the way in which we order the
information we receive. According to the Gregoric model
of learning styles (on which the Tobias book is based),
Gary's dominant learning styles are "Concrete Sequential
and Concrete Random"; mine are "Abstract Sequential
and Abstract Random." We hope our children learn to do
what we are learning to do—understand others, adapt
and accommodate—according to His Word.

Most of us who teach children are aware that learning
is a multisensory experience. And, for all children, especially in the early years, we must focus on those senses
which are working best for them; not that we will neglect
the other senses, but in order that we may help our children find success early in the basic skills. As a reading
specialist, I have watched the world unfold for young
children through tactile-kinesthetic activities. But, the answer is not in allowing children to choose how and what
they will learn, rather it is in finding how young children
are in fact able to learn. As we teach our children, we

learn that the more senses we engage, the more memorable the lesson tends to be.

Children and adults who are weak in one area need to develop their abilities in that area; but it seems only prudent that they learn to capitalize on the ways in which their senses work best for them. We all need to use a variety of methods which sharpen our visual, auditory, and tactile-kinesthetic skills. Many students in classrooms do not have the advantage of hearing books read to them on a regular basis; in some classrooms, teachers do not give many opportunities for writing, for singing, for moving about, and doing tasks in order to learn and to remember. At home we can use all of our senses, routinely and quite naturally. Home educators have a different set of possibilities than do teachers in public and private schools.

The instructional approach at Hillsdale Academy is a "traditional, values-centered, curriculum stressing basic skills and critical analysis."[23] They rely mainly on primary sources, rather than textbooks. In this regard, the *Hillsdale Academy Resource Guide* is a relevant and an invaluable tool for home educators. The Hillsdale curriculum reflects what I believe to be the best qualities of essentialism and perennialism. As essentialists they express 1) a belief in objective truth and absolute values and 2) the conviction that an essential body of knowledge exists which should be transmitted to the next generation. As perennialists they focus on 1) works which have stood the test of time and on 2) primary sources as the means of learning about real people, real ideas, and real events. Commenting on the tradition and spirit of Hillsdale Academy, they describe their commitment to primary resources:

> Teachers would rely mainly on primary sources (classic works of fiction and poetry, biographies, historical documents), rather than on standard school textbooks, which have been subject to oversimplification, historical revisionism, and an obsessive focus on the problems of U.S. society.[24]

They are particularly sensitive to the way in which revisionism is sweeping the field of children's literature. They advise people to purchase the unaltered versions of the books which they recommend, as listed in their bibliography; and to take note of later editions which have been assigned an editor "to bring older works into conformity with current political fashion."[25]

The Hillsdale curriculum is an excellent resource for those educators who have focused on the characteristics of essentialism and perennialism, which I have just outlined. However, I encourage home educators to recognize the opportunities which they have simply by being at home. All of us who are home educators do well to keep our hearts open to a variety of instructional methods and materials. We have the time and the liberty to select and follow many courses of study and to discover and use many methods of instruction.

An Encouraging Word

Do we really need to understand educational philosophy in order to train our children? Perhaps not. However, such an understanding often enables us to unclutter our lives and to prepare ourselves more easily for the tasks at hand. We hope that this chapter will help educators to become wise shoppers in the market of ideas. We hope that by answering the vital questions readers are able to set goals and prioritize their instructional methods and materials. Most of us do not need a great many of the strategies which people are selling. But, we do need to determine which methods and materials will help us to reach our educational goals.

Last year I met a young woman named Melissa, and we have since become close friends. Her story illustrates the message of this chapter. Before I tell the story of her journey as a home educator, I need to say that she and her husband are godly parents whose children are kind, gentle, and teachable. The school-age children are cheerful, disciplined, and accomplished in their studies. And all of the children sparkle with life.

Melissa's oldest daughter, who is now thirteen, attended kindergarten. During their daughter's year in kindergarten, Melissa and her husband decided to become home educators. During her daughter's first year of homeschooling (for first grade) Melissa used everything she could imagine to make her home just like a classroom. She used workbooks, as well as a blackboard, a flag, and a bulletin board—everything which would make home seem like "school." Then, the next year she realized that she did not have to do everything that classroom teachers were doing in order to be a good home educator. She decided that she did not want to bring the school to her home; she wanted to bring her child home to school. Then, when her three daughters were ages seven, four, and six months, Melissa's husband, David, a young man of thirty-three, died. There had been no illness, no warning.

David and his brothers had grown up in the Philippines where their parents served as missionaries. After David's death, his brother Philip left California and moved back to South Carolina, where Melissa and the children lived. Ten months after his brother's death, Phillip told Melissa that he believed that her children needed a father, that she needed a husband, and that the Lord had shown him that it was his responsibility to marry her. Although he had been a wonderful brother-in-law and a dear uncle to her children, the proposal was not what Melissa had in mind. Melissa replied that the key ingredients weren't there—no hearts, no flowers, no music, no falling in love. Just a very godly man who wanted to fulfill his responsibility before God. He shared his heart: he believed that their marriage would be good for the children, and that God would make it wonderful for all of them. And, God did. After they were married, Melissa and Phillip fell quite in love and so they remain. But, on to the details of homeschooling. After Philip and Melissa had been married for two years, Hannah was born. Melissa became pregnant again shortly thereafter and had a miscarriage. Then, two years later, Matt was born. Shortly after Matt's birth, Melissa got pregnant again and had another miscarriage. During these pregnancies and births, Melissa educated her children at home. She used the Bob Jones curriculum and textbooks for each of her daughters in every grade and followed the teacher's guides carefully. She taught all of the subjects they offered except reading. She used *Sing, Spell, Read, Write* to teach each child to read. Her children excelled in their studies. They overcame their grief, and Uncle Philip truly became their dad, a wonderful new dad. By the time their oldest daughter reached sixth grade, Melissa knew that that would be her last year with the textbooks and teacher's manuals. She could not continue physically to do the work which she felt the textbooks and manuals required. Rather than abandon home education, they chose to enroll all of the school-age children in the A Beka video school for all of their subjects. Did she consider it ideal? No. But, she praises God for the quality of the instruction and the way in which her daughters submitted to the new method. During their two years of video instruction, her oldest daughter completed seventh and eighth grade, her second daughter, fourth and fifth grade, and her third daughter, second grade. She became pregnant and delivered her sixth child during the last year in which the children participated in the A Beka video school. Now, she is planning a new and exciting year of homeschooling for the fall of 1995.

What methods will she use now? She believes that the Word of God is the measure of truth and the means for determining what is good and what is evil. She believes that by imparting an essential body of knowledge, her children will better understand our country's background in Western civilization, that they will better understand other areas and other cultures as well. She does not despise textbooks. She praises God for the marvelous materials published by Bob Jones University Press and by A Beka Books. Her children are accomplished scholars, and they have benefited from these educational materials.

As I write this chapter she has begun introducing living books to the children. They have already dropped video school and have begun a new schedule this spring. She plans to use textbooks as resources in the future. She will use the Hirsch series together with several scope and sequence charts; these books will provide a foundation for a curriculum using real books, real life, and real people. The children are excited about working together as a family, doing unit studies and reading aloud. The older girls are glad to be free from the isolation of sitting before a video monitor. For all of them, it is a kind of home coming. But, they have no regrets. Melissa and Phillip believe that living and working together as a family is the greatest benefit they derive from teaching their children at home.

Let us be creative in our own lives, without sitting in judgment concerning the choices which others make. By the Spirit, each of us can find what methods and materials will work for our family. He will make a way.

> The words of wise men are like goads, and masters of these collections are like well-driven nails; they are given by one Shepherd. But beyond this, my son, be warned; the writing of many books is endless, and excessive devotion to books is wearying to the body.
>
> The conclusion, when all has been heard, is: fear God and keep His commandments, because this applies to every person.
>
> For God will bring every act to judgment, everything which is hidden, whether it is good or evil. (Eccles. 12:11–14)

**The Eclectic's Library:
Finding What Works for You**

Strong Elements of Essentialism

Textbook Suppliers

A Beka Textbooks and materials:
A Beka Correspondence School
A Beka Video Home School
A Beka Scope and Sequence Chart–Nursery through
Grade 12
    Bob Jones University Textbooks and Materials

Magazines

The Teaching Home Magazine

Books

The Christian Home School by Gregg Harris
The Home School Manual by Theodore Wade

Strong Elements of Both Essentialism and Perennialism

Curriculum and Reference Guides

Hillsdale Academy Reference Guide

Books

The Core Knowledge Series edited by E.D. Hirsch, Jr.:
What Your First Grader Needs to Know
What Your Second Grader Needs to Know
What Your Third Grader Needs to Know
What Your Fourth Grader Needs to Know
What Your Fifth Grader Needs to Know
What Your Sixth Grader Needs to Know
A First Dictionary of Cultural Literacy: What Your Children Need to Know edited by E.D. Hirsch, Jr.
Cultural Literacy: What Every American Needs to Know by
E.D. Hirsch

Strong Elements of Perennialism

Books for Lifetime Learning

Great Books of the Western World (Volumes One through Fifty-four) edited by Robert Maynard Hutchins

Books About Education

The Original Home Schooling Series, Six Volumes, by Charlotte Mason

For the Children's Sake, Foundations of Education for Home and School by Susan Schaeffer Macaulay

The Closing of the American Mind by Allan Bloom

Guides to Books for Children

Teaching Children: A Curriculum Guide to What Children Need to Know at Each Level Through Sixth Grade by Diane Lopez

Books Children Love: A Guide to the Best Children's Literature by Elizabeth Wilson

Honey for a Child's Heart, The Imaginative Use of Books in Family Life by Gladys Hunt

Read for Your Life by Gladys Hunt

Let the Authors Speak, A Guide to Worthy Books Based on Historical Setting by Carolyn Hatcher

Magazines

The Parents' Review (based on reprints from the original magazine) edited by Charlotte Mason

Catalogues Featuring "Living Books" and "Twaddle-Free" History

Blue Stocking Press, *Educational Spectrums Catalog* by Jane Williams

The Always Incomplete Catalogue, Lifetime Books and Gifts by Bob and Tina Farewell

Greenleaf Press Catalogue by Rob and Cyndy Shearer

Video Curriculum

How Should We Then Live? by Dr. Francis Schaeffer

Strong Elements of Both Perennialism and Progressivism

Books

How to Create Your Own Unit Study by Valerie Bendt
You Can Teach Your Child Successfully by Ruth Beechick

Magazines

Homeschooling Today, Practical Help for Christian Families

Strong Elements of Progressivism

Books

School Can Wait by Raymond and Dorothy Moore
Better Late Than Early by Raymond and Dorothy Moore
Home Grown Kids by Raymond and Dorothy Moore
Home-Spun Schools by Raymond and Dorothy Moore
Homestyle Teaching by Raymond and Dorothy Moore
Homemade Health by Raymond and Dorothy Moore
Homebuilt Discipline by Raymond and Dorothy Moore
Homeschool Burnout by Raymond and Dorothy Moore
The Successful Homeschool Family Handbook, A Creative and Stress-Free Approach to Homeschooling by Raymond and Dorothy Moore

Curriculum

KONOS Unit Study Curriculum and Products by Jessica Huley and Carole Thaxton.
The Weaver Curriculum produced by Becky Avery.

Magazines

Parent Educator and Family Report

Strong Elements of Existentialism

Books

How Children Learn by John Holt
How Children Fail by John Holt
Your Own by John Holt

Learning All the Time by John Holt
Homeschooling For Excellence by David and Micki Colfax

Magazines

Growing Without Schooling
Home Education Magazine

Eclectic

Educational Resource Guides

Christian Home Educator's Curriculum Manual by Cathy Duffy
Vol. One—Grades One through Six
Vol. Two—Grades Seven through Twelve

Magazines

Quit Ye Like Men
Patriarch

Compendious Surveys of Everything Pertaining to Home Learning

Educational Resource Guides

The Big Book of Home Learning, Volumes 1-4 by Mary Pride

Magazines

Practical Homeschooling published by Mary Pride

Ways to Establish an Eclectic Library

Possible funding	*Possible Locations*
Personal income	In the homes of individual home educators
Local Support Group	Shelf space in one of the Sunday school rooms or other rooms at a local church.
Business and Community Leaders	The local public library—on reference shelves or in general circulation

State Support Group

Any church, library, or civic organization willing to provide shelf space or a room for homeschooling materials and willing to give home educators access to the material during regular hours. Such a arrangement may require that materials be kept on reserve, since some people would be driving long distances to review the materials.

Independent Curriculum Consultants

Anyone who is charging money for giving advice ought to have an extensive library available to his/her clients.

The South Carolina Association of Independent Home Schools (SCAIHS) is a nonprofit organization established by the South Carolina legislature to approve and supervise home-schooling drive programs. The number of member-schools in SCAIHS is 880 with an enrollment of 1540 students.

Every member-school has access to the resource room at the SCAIHS offices. The Resource Room is equipped with a large conference table and extensive collection of books, guides, catalogues, and magazines. Parents drive to the offices in Columbia from locations all across the state in order to spend several hours or the entire day in the resource room. The SCAIHS staff is available to parents during business hours Monday through Friday and evenings by appointment. Gaining access to a home-school library has inestimable worth.

Chapter Seven

Finding the Will to Organize Our Time and Material Possessions

There are a number of very good books on the market which can enhance our lives by helping us to declutter our homes and manage our time. But, overcoming a lack of knowledge is not the first challenge we face; the first obstacle which many of us have encountered, at one time or another, is an unwillingness to become faithful stewards of all that God has given us. Only by His grace can we find the will to organize our time and material possessions in ways which minister to those around us and allow us to fulfill our life purpose in Him.

The delight in taking responsibility for organizing my time and material possessions has been, and continues to be, the result of many spiritual awakenings. I personally underwent a supernatural transformation during the first two years of my marriage to Gary. I came to realize that I regarded some work as important and other work as menial. I saw no value in menial work; I took no pleasure in it; I avoided it. But, nowhere in the Word of God are we told to consider work in that way. When we work as unto Him, it becomes His work. And, He is glorified when we yield everything we touch to Him. And, the great news is that we have the power in Him to do so because we are made "alive in Christ" according to Ephesians 2:4–7. Every thought, word, and deed is part of who we are in Him, "who raised us up with Him and seated us with Him in the heavenly places, in Christ Jesus"!

He is Lord of our day, all of our day, with all of the duties, responsibilities, pleasures, and pain. We cannot teach our children His ways until His ways are our own. And, we cannot teach our children to praise God for whatever He sets their hands to do, until we have learned that ourselves. "Whatever you do, do your work heartily as for the Lord rather than for men; knowing that from the Lord you will receive the reward of the inheritance. It is the Lord Christ whom you serve" (Col. 3:23–24).

This chapter is not about how to organize our time and material possessions; but, rather, it is about 1) considering why we may be, or may have been, reluctant to organize our time and material possessions and 2) finding the will to submit to God, asking Him to cause us to want to do that which we have been unwilling or reluctant to do.

I can testify of God's mercy in my own life in dealing with my weaknesses in this area. In graduate school, in my church, and as a college professor, I had what I considered to be a very active, productive life. I had been a widow for nearly two years before Gary and I married. Nothing in my life until that point had prepared me for the real business, the godly business, of being a keeper at home. It wasn't until months after Gary and I married that I recognized that I had no heart for the homemaking tasks at hand. I did not value what I now know to be an essential part of life. Through a very painful time of trial, I came to recognize my own worldliness. Before that I thought of worldliness in terms of dress, preferences in music and entertainment, and I did not consider myself a carnally minded Christian. But, the Lord revealed my heart through His Word. Proverbs 31 and Titus 2 outline the wide range of womanly tasks which God designed to satisfy our hearts. He counts as precious many of the activities which I considered insignificant. However, I learned that the home is an oasis of blessing when the Lord sets it in order.

When Christian men, women, and children manage their time and material possessions by His Spirit, they are sensitive to the needs of others, especially those within their own household. Productivity in the eyes of the world is not God's standard for organization. The Proverbs woman "looks well to the ways of her household, and does not eat the bread of idleness" (Prov. 31:27).

The Apostle Paul offers us the most thorough and vivid explanation of how we are to regard the work He sets before us. He is clearly the model for us as we decide what we will do with the challenges before us. This is a wonderful passage to remember when we believe we cannot endure our responsibilities any longer. We learn from Paul what it is to be a good steward of everything He gives to us—especially the challenges. Paul accepted the stewardship of God's challenges just as he chose to be a good steward of his time and material possessions. Challenges are assets in the heart of God.

> To this present hour we are both hungry and thirsty, and are poorly clothed, and are roughly treated, and are homeless; and we toil, working with our own hands; when we are reviled, we bless; when we are persecuted, we endure; when we are slandered, we try to conciliate; we have become as the scum of the world, the dregs of all things, even until now. I do not write these things to shame you, but to admonish you as my beloved children. For if you were to have countless tutors in Christ, yet you would not have many fathers; for in Christ Jesus I became your father through the gospel. I exhort you therefore, be imitators of me. (1 Cor. 10–16)

During the first few weeks that Gary and I were married, he wanted to organize everything about our lives at home. He was vitally concerned about the laundry—how it would be done, who would do it, and when it would be done; he wanted to discuss meals—when would they be served, who would serve them, who would plan them, who would prepare them; he wanted to schedule the events and people in our lives. Through the Word of God, I recognized my own need, the need to come home, and to discover what the Lord would have me to do there. I resigned my teaching position at the University of Miami and began a new life.

I did not change all of my attitudes and behaviors overnight, but in response to His prompting—as well as, His chastisement—I began to think about the details of my life quite differently. Important activities energized me; bothersome activities slowed me down. Through the Word of God, I set a new standard for what I would count as important and what might prove to be bothersome. Until Gary and I married, I had thought of myself as hard working, diligent, responsible, and disciplined—and I was, in all of the areas that pleased me.

I praise God with all of my heart for the fiery ordeal which characterized our first two years of married life. Our responses to failure and His mercy toward us transformed our lives. First, we recognized our need to know Christ and to be changed by the power of His Word; secondly, we purposed to live within limited means financially in order that I might stay at home; and finally, we asked God for children, as many as He chose according to His will to give to us. The Lord gave us four children in five years. I was thirty-six when our first child was born in 1983, and I was forty-one when our last child was born. As I look back on that time when the children were five and under and seven and under, I realize that limited financial resources caused us to simplify our lives. I learned during those precious years all that I now treasure concerning the value of every task at hand. The Lord showed me how to look to the ways of my household and to find richness and fulfillment in every area of life. Books and papers still played a part, but only a part. I learned that the very act of keeping the home clean and in order gives meaning and dignity to the activities that occur in the home. To be sure, my standard of clean and orderly is not always the same as my husband's; after thirteen years, we are both still in process. But, our goals are the same and our hearts beat as one in this matter.

The way in which we keep the few or many areas of our homes reveals our attitude about the work and the business of life which goes on there. Kitchens and bathrooms are important places. Essential items must be cleaned and stored in an orderly fashion if we are to function well in those areas. How we leave each room of our home and how we find each room touches our lives. Doing our work heartily as unto the Lord does not mean that we will each do our work as well as another or with the same sensitivity. It is the intention of our heart that counts. And, we must allow both adults and children to grow in tasks, as He enables them. Otherwise, the fruit of the Spirit cannot abound in us.

My father-in-law is an engineer, a musician, a gardener, a painter—a man with many talents and gifts. When my mother-in-law became ill, he did the vacuuming and cleaning and cooking—effortlessly. Of course, it was work, but he did everything well. Now, he is in a wonderful retirement center. He has resumed his organ lessons, attends all lectures and events, and is in charge of coordinating the activities in his unit. And, I am married to his son. Gary can build, repair, and remodel buildings. He can fix nearly anything that breaks. He assisted his father with the lawn care and gardening even as a small child. Gary believes you have to understand laundry, and he irons beautifully. Although he doesn't do the cooking and cleaning, he certainly can. This is the person whom God assigned as my personal trainer. But, just after we were married, I believed that God had assigned him to be my personal tormentor. Little did I know that he was feeling the same way. Gary had to learn that acceptance cannot be based on performance, and I had to learn that His love causes us to perform, unselfishly, to the best of our ability.

Just after our second child was born, I couldn't imagine anyone having a fuller day than I. I was nursing both children at that time. Reading, walking, playing, tending, feeding, cooking, cleaning, sleeping, and other essentials filled each day. Each of those tasks represented a new learning curve, and I had no mentor, no tutor. Gary did the laundry, maintained the house and grounds, and ran his own business. I planned never to write anything of any length until my sixties or seventies (depending upon how many children we finally had). I could never have imagined back then the life that now seems to me as balanced, normal, and complete. What we learned in the last decade is that living with our children, not just as parents and teachers, but as fellow learners allows us all to enjoy the journey. When we as parents stop learning and doing new things, we lose the capacity to empathize with our children. As our children watch us learn new information or ideas and attempt new tasks—by the power of the Spirit—they come to view learning as a delightful and integral part of living. Organizing our time and material possessions is essential business. If we lack the skills we need or lack the will to learn the skills we need— the Lord will change us by the power of the blood that raised Christ from the dead. We "can do all things through Him who strengthens" us (Phil. 4:13).

I have friends across the country who are home educators, precious, talented women of God, whose lives are in many ways handicapped because they lack the will to organize their time and material possessions. For some of them, their home businesses are overwhelming; for others, the number of small children in the family requires more time and energy than they can imagine ever having; for others, many others, meals, laundry, and housework get lost in their panic to focus on "school." And, in every case that comes to mind, the husbands are servants of God. They are gentle, kind-hearted men. But, true love must also confront, challenge, and propose a solution in Christ. Many husbands do take the lead and press for change. The heartfelt cry of the following appeal can bring liberation to an entire family:

> We are handicapped as a family because we are not
> organizing our time and material possessions in
> ways that glorify God. And we are passing these
> handicaps on to our children. We cannot live this
> way. We must submit to God's will for our lives and
> walk in obedience. He will change us if we are
> willing to be changed. Dear, Lord, make us willing.

I can say without a doubt that without God's chastisement in my life during my first two years of marriage to
Gary and at critical junctures since that time—and into
the present—my life would be in chaos. Gary and I shared
our testimony with a very sweet, southern lady who had
commented graciously about how well we all worked together in our home. He quickly told her how very differently things had been when he and I were first married.
"Why Gary," she exclaimed after hearing some of the
more lively details, "you were right mean." Oh, yes, I'll
attest to that. He was downright mean. The Lord used
our "meanness" as His means of breaking both Gary's will
and mine. Then, as the Lord showed me His truth concerning marriage and family, I knew that I could not find
my way without His hand. He leads us into light and
clarity. The very essence of my life now—all that I hold
most dear—has come through Christ. He equips us to do
what He calls us to do.

> Now the God of peace, who brought up from the
> dead the great Shepherd of the sheep through the
> blood of the eternal covenant, even Jesus our Lord,
> equip you in every good thing to do His will, work-
> ing in us that which is pleasing in His sight, through
> Jesus Christ, to whom be the glory forever and
> ever. Amen. (Heb. 13:20)

I identify with those who are struggling, whose lives
are in slow motion, for whom homeschooling is a real
stretch. The Lord gives us time to grow. When I think of
where Gary and I were, just a decade ago, one incident
speaks volumes. One morning, in Florida, in the winter

of 1985, when Canaan was six or seven months old, I stepped into the garage and threw a load of laundry into the washer. I returned to the kitchen where I was attending to something in the early morning. Gary was still in bed asleep. Suddenly, I heard pounding in the garage, as though someone were inside the washing machine trying to get out. Going into the garage to discover what had happened to the machine did not occur to me—that was basically unfamiliar territory. I ran to the bedroom to alert Gary. "Gary, wake up! There's a hammering inside the washing machine. It's really loud!" He moaned and rolled over in a dead sleep. Then, he bolted upright. I could see the whites of his eyes. He screamed, "The minibasket!" He leaped out of bed and ran to the garage. I followed him, amazed that even in his sleep he could unfold this mystery. The noise had stopped by the time I got to the garage. "What happened?" I asked. "I turned the machine off," he answered calmly. "But the noise, what caused the noise?" He looked at me in bewilderment, "Terry, didn't you notice that the minibasket was in the machine when you loaded all the laundry in it. Didn't you notice that the dial was set for the minibasket?" Of course I didn't. The function, care, and control of the minibasket had never entered my mind. "Gary," I exclaimed, "the way you tore out of the bedroom, I thought maybe the whole end of the house was going to explode!" He just stood there, staring at me. Then, suddenly, I burst out laughing. I couldn't quit laughing for a very long time, and he finally laughed too. Before we "put on a heart of compassion, kindness, humility, gentleness and patience: bearing with one another, and forgiving each other," (Col. 3:12,13) we usually learn to laugh.

Finding the Will

Life is full of connecting moments, and, if we have the mind of Christ and the joy of the Lord, we will grasp the significance in them all. But, we don't deal creatively with the work set before us until we accept it and embrace it as from Him. Just as we need to answer the vital questions and to establish goals based on those answers, before we choose instructional methods and materials, we need also to examine our major goals carefully in order to understand the work ahead of us. If the goals are of Him, then He will supply the strength to accomplish them. As Gary and I examine and reexamine each of our five major goals, we consider the work load involved in accomplishing our goals. We find the will to achieve our goals by confessing our weaknesses, faults, and failures; by asking the Lord to meet our specific needs; and by proclaiming to Him and to each other, His faithfulness.

Educational Goals and the Effort Required to Achieve Each Goal

Our Family Goals

Goal

1. Lead the family in personal devotions, family devotions and family worship, and Bible study in order that by His Spirit these activities will have preeminence in our lives.

Challenges

Set a time for personal devotions and family worship and ask God to make us diligent.

Recognize that late nights interfere with early mornings.

Remember that these activities are the main objectives for the day and that we will allot as much time to other activities as we are able.

Help the children find personal messages from their reading of the Word, by sharing the personal messages we have received.

Make certain that the kitchen and living room are left in order the night before, so that family devotions and family worship can begin on time.

Ask the children to discuss personal devotions, family worship and Bible study in their daily journal.

Pray faithfully that God would speak to each of our hearts during our personal devotions, family worship, and Bible study.

Serve as biblical role models by being faithful in our hearts and minds and actions to do all that we ask and expect from the children.

Praise God for His blessing upon this time with Him.

Goal

2. Read the good books and the great books aloud to our children, acknowledging that by doing this we will greatly improve the quality of each of our lives. And, set aside a time for silent reading in addition to any reading for pleasure which we may do.

Challenges

Enjoy the time spent in reading aloud and count the time set aside for it as precious.

Make time during or after meals for reading something of interest to everyone.

Always be involved in some book and share something about it during one of the family meetings during the day.

Encourage everyone to discuss the interesting books which they are reading during conversations throughout the day with individuals or with the entire group.

Keep all library books in a designated place and put library days on the calendar.

Take time for the great books as the Lord leads because they are worth the effort.

Enter books, people, and ideas of great note on the timeline using symbols of interest to the children.

Keep track of library sales and allow the children to build their own personal libraries.

Be certain that every child keeps a record of worthy books in his/her reading notebook.

Set aside a time for silent reading when everyone is involved in silent reading.

Goal

3. Use textbooks, reference books, and a variety of educational resources as tools which assist in organizing the great ideas and which inspire us to consider and reconsider them; but never use textbooks or other educational materials as substitutions for the original unabridged writings of the authors themselves.

Challenges

Keep ample textbooks, reference books, and other educational resources on special shelves for each child.

Continue to use textbooks as they are needed to supplement the reading which each child is doing.

Explain, from time to time, how textbooks are arranged in our home library according to subjects, rather than grade levels.

Set aside some part of every week just to sit together and examine educational resources (e.g., finding information about some person, event, or idea from twenty different sources).

Do a research project once a quarter using the Greenville, South Carolina library.

Make regular comparisons between the textbook treatment of certain ideas (e.g., the ideas and attitudes of the American Founding Fathers) and the words of the authors themselves as found in the primary sources (diaries, journals, letters, and state papers).

Provide regular examples of the way in which history is being revised. Be on the alert for textbook give-a-ways which are available in many states. Evaluate textbooks regularly in order that the children may learn to analyze the ways in which information is presented. Note the differences between Christian textbooks and government school textbooks.

Encourage filing and sorting activities by allowing time for everyone to organize their boxes (as big as laundry baskets). Keep school papers in notebooks, pencils in boxes, letters in files, etc.

Goal

4. Organize time and material possessions in ways that allow each of the disciplines of life—the life skills, fine arts, liberal arts, computational skills, and communications skills—to impact our growth and development as a family.

Life Skills/Challenges

Allow the children to divide household tasks among themselves as much as possible and encourage team work.

Demonstrate the way in which tasks are done at regular intervals until each individual has mastered each particular job.

Prepare meals and clean-up afterward as a group much of the time in order to enjoy family fellowship during routine activities.

Demonstrate peace and contentment while working alone at household tasks by praising God for the time to think, listen, sing, and to be still.

Be certain that the children demonstrate competency in each of the household tasks in which they are a part (as their ages and abilities allow). Always affirm their efforts to do the same tasks in better ways or different ways.

Allow the children to take responsibility for planning meals according to guidelines for health and nutrition which they have learned.

Set aside time for each child to take part in food preparation in order that each child will learn to take care of himself/herself and others.

Set aside time for each child to take part in the milling and baking activities and be certain that each child fully understands and can articulate the advantages and the health benefits connected with home food systems.

Take delight in the contributions which each family member makes and praise God for the blessings of the family.

Set aside time for each member of the family to organize and eliminate (if necessary) personal property.

Set aside time to organize and eliminate (if necessary) material possessions in the common areas.

Reorganize and de-clutter book shelves and supply boxes at the end of each day's activities.

Remain enthusiastic about the ways in which everyone helps to make the home such a pleasant place to be.

Fine Arts/Challenges

Request fine arts calendars from the local college campuses, and select concerts and art shows that would be meaningful.

Purchase a season ticket for the Bob Jones University Concert and Drama Series, and prepare each quarter for the coming events.

Purpose to attend some of the Bob Jones University vespers programs on Sunday afternoon.

Draw with the children several times a week.

Allow time for the family to listen to classical music written by the composers which we are studying.

Explore the fine arts each quarter by visiting the local museums, galleries, and libraries in the area.

Liberal Arts/Challenges

Use the *Core Knowledge Series*, Scope and Sequence Charts from various publishers, and the *Hillsdale Academy Reference Guide* in order to plan which living books and great books we will be reading together and which ones each child will read silently.

Articulate the ways in which particular family readings are enriching our lives. Also share the inspiration and pleasure which we as parents have received from the books we are currently reading.

Talk about the individual authors who have written some of the great books of the Western world as their lives and ideas relate to certain studies and conversations.

Remember that ideas are interesting and exciting when we understand them. Keep training the children to think and to analyze the words which they hear read or spoken or which they read.

Encourage every member of the family to share thoughts and ideas and to discuss the topics which are interesting, challenging, perplexing, or upsetting.

Computational Skills/Challenges

Continue to discuss with friends and acquaintances the educational methods and materials which they have found or are finding helpful.

Take particular note of each child's progress and recognize achievement.

Remember that simply because one child responds favorably to a math series doesn't mean that the other children will respond in the same way.

Set aside time for the children to examine educational resources at curriculum fairs, bookstores, and libraries.

Set specific goals and work toward mastering concepts.

Discover what each child needs.

Find ways to meet each child's needs by offering 1) more time from both parents in this area of instruction, 2) additional educational materials, 3) other methods such as computer programs and video classes.

Communications Skills/Challenges

Continue to integrate reading, writing, speaking, and listening skills into all of the activities throughout the course of each day.

Be certain that the younger children, as well as the older ones, understand the value of a systematized presentation of phonics. Be certain that every child has a sure foundation in phonics, a method for independent word attack. Be certain that the younger children understand the difference between decoding and the complex process that we call reading.

Offer every possible opportunity for enrichment in verbal communications every day. Daily activities should include opportunities to read, speak, write, and listen: reading aloud, listening to books being read aloud (parents reading or performers on tape); speaking to the family or to a group; conversing about books and ideas; retelling a story or summarizing books, information, and ideas; writing in a daily journal; writing a letter or letters. Set aside ample time to listen to stories, conversations, the Scripture, and prayers.

Goal

5. Live with our children as fellow learners.

Challenges

Walk by the power of the Spirit in order that we may not become distracted by the many demands upon our lives to learn, and to do, and to learn to do.

Allow our children, through prayer and family worship, to understand the way in which God changes our lives.

Read, write, speak, and listen in their presence throughout the day in order that the children will have an ever-present model of those activities.

Where do we find the will to do what we need to do? Where do we find the time to do what we need to do? Where do we find the ability to do what we need to do? Where do we find the energy to do what we need to do? In Christ. If we are lead by the Spirit, we are empowered by the Spirit. As our hearts burn with convictions and as He gives us a vision for our homes, we are able to set goals which will energize us, rather than oppress us. What do we do when we get off course—for a day, a week, a month? We look to Him who set the course and who is the means by which we will complete it. All of us need to give the Word of God preeminence in our lives if we are to achieve any of our goals. And, if His Word has preeminence, then many, many paths are possible in Him. Our major objectives will not be the same. But, for all of us, goals offer us challenges, not condemnation. If we attempt nothing for God, we accomplish less than nothing.

If we attempt nothing for God, even what we do have will
be taken away. The Lord makes this clear in the parable
of the talents (Matt. 25:14–30). The one who attempts
nothing is called a "worthless slave" (Matt. 25:30). But,
what does He offer those who try and fail? Mercy. This is
where we find the will to do what we need to do—in the
mercy of God!

> He has not dealt with us according to our sins, Nor
> rewarded us according to our iniquities, For as high
> as the heavens are above the earth, So great is His
> lovingkindness toward those who fear Him. As far
> as the east is from the west, So far has He removed
> our transgressions from us. Just as a father has
> compassion on his children, So the Lord has com-
> passion on those who fear Him. For He Himself
> knows our frame; He is mindful that we are but
> dust. (Ps. 103:10–14)

And if we are wise, we find our will to do that which
we need to do in the fear of the Lord. The psalmist
promises His lovingkindness on those who fear Him. He
also promises us that the Lord has compassion on those
who fear Him. Does He expect us to stay on course without Him? No, indeed we dare not, for He is our strength.
"He is mindful that we are but dust" (Ps. 103:14).

We will find our will to do that which we need to do
by growing in Christian virtue. And, we grow by purpos-
ing to be about our Father's business. When we are involved in His business, we learn to eliminate distractions.
Peter tells us exactly how we may find the will to be useful
and fruitful and to grow in virtue. Our Lord has granted
us everything pertaining to life and godliness. We are
partakers of His divine nature (2 Pet. 3, 4).

> Now for this very reason also, applying all dili-
> gence, in your faith supply moral excellence, and
> in your moral excellence knowledge; and in your
> knowledge, self-control, and in your self-control,
> perseverance, and in your perseverance, godliness;

and in your godliness, brotherly kindness, and in your brotherly kindness, love.

For if these qualities are yours and are increasing they render you neither useless nor unfruitful in the true knowledge of our Lord Jesus Christ. (2 Pet. 1:5–8)

Chapter Eight

Overcoming Fear of Failure

Our Attitude toward Success and Failure[1]

When we are hindered by our previous failures and when we are encouraged by our own abilities, we are living in the realm of the law. Human strength, intelligence, and talent count for nothing in the kingdom of God. According to 1 Corinthians 1:26–31, He did not call many who were wise according to the flesh, not many mighty, not many noble.

> But God has chosen the foolish things of the world to shame the wise, and God has chosen the weak things of the world to shame the things which are strong. . . . But by His doing you are in Christ Jesus, who became to us wisdom from God, and righteousness and sanctification, and redemption, that, just as it is written, "Let him who boasts, boast in the Lord." (1 Cor. 1:27, 30, 31)

If we agonize over whether or not we can do—in and of ourselves—that which we know we need to do, according to the Word of God, then we are under the curse of the law. When I consider the words I have written in the previous chapters, the main objectives which my husband and I have established and the challenges we face, I declare that we will trust in the lovingkindness and the mercy of God. Do any of us imagine that the children in our care will grow strong in the Lord by the wisdom, power, and might which is within us. The image the psalmist gives to us as parents is one which we as parents understand so well. He describes the composed and quieted soul of a child who is weaned resting against his mother. We as parents are to have that same childlike trust in God. "O, Lord, my heart is not proud, nor my eyes haughty; Nor do I involve myself in great matters, Or in things too difficult for me" (Ps. 131:1).

The safety, security, training, education, and eternal destiny of our children are matters too great for us! We are foolish or mad if we imagine that there is hope in anything but God. Paul's tone seems to be one of exasperation when he deals with the Galatians in this matter: "Are you so foolish?" Paul asks them—and us (Gal. 3:3). When we are facing the fear of failure, that is the question which we need to ask ourselves, "Are we so foolish?" Why do we trust in the flesh for anything? For, when we see Christ, we lose all confidence in the flesh! That is, when we have a revelation of Christ, we don't count on the flesh to serve us for good or for ill.

> For through the law I died to the law that I might
> live to God. I have been crucified with Christ; and
> it is no longer I who live, but Christ lives in me;
> and the life which I now live in the flesh I live by
> faith in the Son of God, who loved me, and delivered Himself up for me. (Gal. 2:19, 20)

When we live under the law, we emphasize the things that we are doing; when we are in Christ, we recognize the things which we are seeing Him do. The Law is condemning, while faith is redeeming.

How do we as parents deal with forgiveness? Do we quickly restore relationships? Have our children learned to forgive and to seek restoration? Those who are under the law are condemning; they believe that people don't deserve to be forgiven.

Are we as parents easily frustrated? Are our children easily frustrated? Those who are under the law become angry and resentful with others who don't perform as well as they expect—just as they become angry with themselves in response to frustration. Those who are living in performance, do not believe that they deserve whatever ill befalls them.

Do we reject other believers who have different standards? Or, do we walk in accordance with Romans 14? Those who are under the law do not stand in the liberty of Christ. They are bound and not free. Those who walk in the realm of the law are filled with frustration, pride, and arrogance. They are angry people.

> Christ redeemed us from the curse of the Law, having become a curse for us—for it is written, "Cursed is everyone who hangs on a tree"—in order that in Christ Jesus the blessing of Abraham might come to the Gentiles, so that we might receive the promise of the Spirit through faith. (Gal. 3:13–14)

Servants of Christ, Stewards of the Mysteries of God

Everything we are rests on our identity in Christ. If we know who we are in Him, who the Word says we are in Him, then we are secure. We have no fear. However, if we have an identity which is based on the opinions of those around us (e.g., parents, friends, relatives), or on the ideas of the world (e.g., the government or news media), or on our own opinions (a good self-image or a bad self-image), then we are deceived concerning our identity.

Who are we? We are servants of Christ, stewards of the mysteries of God. And, no matter what the people around us believe, or what the world thinks, or what we think about ourselves, we belong to Him. All that concerns us is in His hands. Scheduling time, organizing events and people, teaching and deciding what to teach— these are matters too great for us. God has all of the information, all of the answers. We are secure in Christ Jesus our Lord.

If our identity is in man, we walk in condemnation and judgment. We must examine our lives for signs of insecurity. When we are walking in the curse of the law, we are insecure. If the answers to these questions reveal our suffering and insecurity, we can run to the Rock. When our heart is faint, He will hear our cry from the end of the earth (Ps. 61:2, 3)!

Are we critical of everyone and everything? Are we always evaluating the behaviors of others? Are we perfectionists? Do we set the world's standard in whatever categories we choose? Do we isolate ourselves? Are we defensive when we are confronted? Are we controlling in the lives of others? Must we shape the reality around ourselves? Must we dominate thoughts, events, activities, outcomes? Are we catering to addictions in order to satisfy our emptiness? How do we regard food, clothing, recreation, money, work—and everything else in our lives? Are we anxious? Are we eating too much, talking too much, laughing too much—is any otherwise normal activity out of balance?

We are delivered from the bondage of insecurity if we are in Him. "There is now no condemnation for those who are in Christ Jesus" (Rom. 8:1). "For the law of the Spirit of life in Christ Jesus has set you free from the law of sin and death" (Rom. 8:2). If the concern of our lives is what other people think about us or what we think about ourselves, we will wrestle with insecurity, and we will never overcome a fear of failure. But, if we are concerned about the Lord, the One who is unchanging, we will overcome our fear of failure. Proverbs 29:25 tells us that the fear of man brings a snare, but that whosoever trusts in the Lord will be saved.

Faith and the Faithfulness of God

If we had nothing else to read except the book of Psalms and the Book of Hebrews, chapter 11, we would know how to walk without fear. The psalmist tell us of God's lovingkindness, mercy, faithfulness, goodness, holiness, power, gentleness, majesty, and love. The Word tells us that whoever believes in Him will not be disappointed. He has given us every promise, every assurance. He has made a covenant with us. He has given us His Word. The Word of God, from Genesis to Revelation, dispels fear. As we worship God with our families and meet the Lord individually, we will not be afraid. By reading Hebrews 11 aloud together, we can remind ourselves that faith is indeed the victory that overcomes the world. As the stories of these saints fill our minds and touch our hearts, we will not grow weary and lose heart (Heb. 12:1).

Homeschooling is a work, and a good work, if it is His. We are His stewards and His servants. He makes every provision for our lives. The Lord provides us with the Spirit and works miracles among us as we hear with faith (Gal. 3:5). May God give us ears to hear and eyes to see as we read His word.

> Therefore, since we have so great a cloud of witnesses surrounding us, let us also lay aside every encumbrance, and the sin which so easily entangles us, and let us run with endurance the race that is set before us, fixing our eyes on Jesus, the author and perfecter of faith, who for the joy set before him endured the cross, despising the shame, and has sat down at the right hand of the throne of God. (Heb. 12:1–2)

Making Ourselves Available to God[1]

After God attracted Moses' attention with the burning bush, He called Moses to go on a specific mission for Him. At the time the Lord spoke to him, Moses, an eighty-year-old shepherd, was pasturing the flock of his father-in-law, Jethro, the priest of Midian. From the standpoint of anyone in Moses' position, the assignment is incredible: "Therefore, come now, and I will send you to Pharaoh, so that you may bring My people, the sons of Israel out of Egypt" (Exod. 3:10).

Moses felt insecure and insufficient; he didn't want to go. We can understand that. The assignment posed a staggering challenge. For Moses to go to Pharaoh, unarmed, and bring the people out of Egypt was not simply a daring feat, it was undoable. Moses did not express gratitude for being honored in this way. He did not count it a blessing to be used by God to deliver Israel. His answer to the Lord is incredibly focused: "Who am I, that I should go to Pharaoh, and that I should bring the sons of Israel out of Egypt?" (Exod. 3:11).

He couldn't imagine himself doing what God asked him to do. Nor could we—in the flesh. The natural mind cannot imagine a man in Moses' position setting off on such a mission. And, isn't God good to give us those details. Because throughout all of recorded history God has given His people such missions—tasks which are undoable. But, on this occasion the entire conversation concerning the assignment is recorded in the Word of God.

Moses, who actually spoke to the Lord in the burning bush, argued with the Lord about the assignment—and lived to part the Red Sea! Who is this God we serve? We cannot comprehend His goodness and mercy! But, we must believe in His goodness and mercy if we are His. Moses had the burning bush, but we have the Book, the revelation of God to man, the record of God's power and His faithfulness.

Moses' five responses to the Lord are the responses which most of us would make if someone asked us to do a task for which we were totally unfit and unprepared. They are also responses which many servants of God make when examining the call of God on their lives. Because God's pattern is predictable, He gives us assignments which are undoable. Exodus chapters 3 and 4 have a wonderful message to Christians who are home educators or who are contemplating home education. Here are our children (His people) trapped in the world system (in Egypt), and here we are as parents (His servants, stewards of His mysteries) called to lead them out of bondage and into the land of milk and honey. Moses' response to the call on his life reflects the insufficiency and insecurity which many of us feel.

How do we know that anyone can homeschool? We know because God is the God of the impossible. Never mind those who imagine that they can homeschool their children in their own strength; *God calls people who know that they cannot do it in their own strength, who know that they are no match for the power and the might of Egypt.* Those who believe that their children would prosper by being homeschooled, but who also know that they are not fit and not prepared, can be certain of God's call on their lives. He calls us to do the very things which we are unfit and unprepared to do. Most of us know that we are as unfit and unprepared to teach our children at home as Moses was to bring God's people out of Israel. Moses identified every insufficiency he had; God replied with His sufficiency.

Lack of Status

> Moses: Who am I that I should go to Pharaoh? (Exod. 3:11)

> God: Certainly I will be with you, and this shall be the sign to you that it is I who have sent you: when you have brought the people out of Egypt, you shall worship God at this mountain. (Exod. 3:12)

Nothing depended upon Moses. Everything depended upon God.

Lack of Knowledge

> Moses: What will I say when they ask me who you are? Who are you? (Exod. 3:13)

> God: I am who I am. Thus you shall say to the sons of Israel, I am has sent me to you. (Exod. 3:14)

God has complete knowledge. He tells us who He is and what He will do.

Lack of Credibility

> Moses: What if they will not believe me or listen to what I say? For they may say, "The Lord has not appeared to you." (Exod. 4:1)

> God: What is in your hand? (Exod. 4:2)

God will use what we already have, what He has already given us. In His power is our sufficiency.

Lack of Qualifications

> Moses: Please, Lord, I have never been eloquent, neither recently nor in time past, nor since Thou hast spoken to Thy servant; for I am slow of speech and slow of tongue. (Exod. 4:10)

> God: Who has made man's mouth? Or who makes him dumb or deaf, or seeing or blind? Is it not I, the Lord? Now then go, and I, even I, will be with

your mouth, and teach you what you are to say.
(Exod. 4:11–12)

God uses us when we are quiet and totally dependent
upon Him. In Psalm 131, as we mentioned in the last
chapter, the psalmist conveys a childlike trust in the Lord:
"Surely I have composed and quieted my soul; Like a
weaned child rests against his mother, My soul is like a
weaned child within me."

Lack of Confidence

Moses: I am afraid. (Exod. 4:13)

God: (The anger of the Lord burned against Moses.)
Is there not your brother Aaron the Levite? I know
that he speaks fluently. And moreover, behold, he
is coming out to meet you; when he sees you he will
be glad in his heart. And you are to speak to him
and put the words in his mouth; and I, even I, will
be with your mouth and his mouth, and I will teach
you what you are to do. Moreover, he shall speak
for you to the people; and it shall come about that
he shall be as a mouth for you, and you shall be as
God to him. And you shall take in your hand this
staff, with which you shall perform the signs. (Exod.
4:14–17)

He is faithful. If we know our God, we will never lack
confidence. For He has already performed His work. "For
we are His workmanship, created in Christ Jesus for good
works, which God prepared beforehand, that we should
walk in them" (Eph. 2:10).

May We Think His Thoughts

Now to Him who is able to do exceeding abun-
dantly beyond all that we ask or think, according to
the power that works within us, to Him be the glory
in the church and in Jesus Christ to all generations
forever and ever. Amen. (Eph. 3:20–21)

Exploring Instructional Methods and Materials

Books

The Closing of the American Mind by Allan Bloom

The Closing of the American Heart, What's Really Wrong With America's Schools by Ronald H. Nash

Honey for a Child's Heart: The Imaginative Use of Books in Family Life by Gladys M. Hunt

Read for Your Life: Turning Teens into Readers by Gladys Hunt and Barbara Hampton

Books Children Love: A Guide to the Best in Children's Literature by Jane A. Williams

Cultural Literacy: What Every American Needs to Know by E.D. Hirsch

For the Children's Sake, Foundations of Education for Home and School by Susan Schaeffer Macaulay

The Original Home Schooling Series, Six Volumes by Charlotte Mason

Teaching Children: A Curriculum Guide to What Children Need to Know at Each Level through Sixth Grade by Diane Lopez

Let the Authors Speak, A Guide to Worthy Books Based on Historical Setting by Carolyn Hatcher

The Book of Virtues, A Treasury of Great Moral Stories by William Bennett

Catalogues

The Charlotte Mason Research and Supply Company
P.O. Box 172
Stanton, NJ 08885

The Greenleaf Press
1570 Old LaGuardo Road
Lebannon, TN 37087
(615) 475-7500

The Elijah Company
P.O. Box 12483
Knoxville, TN 37912-0483
(615) 475-7500

Beautiful Feet Books
88 West Bradford Avenue
Sonora, CA 95370
(800) 889-1978

Lifetime Books and Gifts (*The Always Incomplete Catalog*)
3900 Chalet Suzanne Drive
Lake Wales, FL 33853-7763
(800) 377-0390

Timberdoodle Company
E 1510 Spencer Lake Road
Shelton, WA 98584

Resource Guides

The Home School Manual, Plans, Pointers, Reasons and Resources
by Theodore E. Wade, Jr., et al.

Christian Home Educator's Curriculum Manual, Volumes 1 and 2
by Cathy Duffy

How to Create Your Own Unit Study by Valerie Bendt

Resource Guide and Compendious Survey of Everything Pertaining to Home Learning

The Big Book of Home Learning, Volumes 1–4 by Mary Pride

Christian Homeschooling Magazines

The Teaching Home
P.O. Box 20219
Portland, OR 97220
(503) 253-9633

Practical Homeschooling
Home Life
P.O. Box 1250
Fenton, MO 63026-1850
(800) 346-6322

Homeschooling Today
P.O. Box 1425
Melrose, FL 32666
(904) 475-3088

The Parents' Review
P.O. Box 172
Stanton, NJ 08885
(503) 461-2816

Quit Ye Like Men
10281 County Road 701
Ripley, MS 38663-9431
(601) 837-4596

Patriarch
P.O. Box 725
Rolla, MO 65401

Other Magazines

Growing Without Schooling
2269 Massachusetts Avenue
Cambridge, MA 02140

Testing

Bob Jones University Press, Testing and Evaluation Service
Greenville, SC 29614-0062

National Home-Education Conventions and Curriculum Fairs

Home Education Leadership Program

The annual five-day H.E.L.P. Conference is one example of the commitment that Bob Jones University has made to home educators. Each year the conference features nationally known guest speakers. Seminars and workshops are conducted by home-educating parents and by members of the BJU staff and faculty. Over 150 different workshops are offered during each conference. Participants have ample time to interact with other parents, and many parents return year after year to do just that.

Child care, day camp, and teen camp are available throughout the week. All children are involved in a wonderful variety of activities, which include chapel time, stories, crafts, games, music, and more. Teens are involved in challenging camp services and a week of exciting and fun games. For information concerning this event contact Conference Coordinator, (803) 242-5100, Extension 4207, or write Bob Jones University, Greenville, South Carolina 29614- 0001.

The Advanced Training Institute

This program is an annual training conference which is available only to those who are members of the Advanced Training Institute (ATI). Both parents must have attended Bill Gothard's Institute in Basic Life Principles in order to become members of ATI; attending a one-week conference (held in Knoxville during June 1995) is also a requirement for membership in ATI. Many parents find the five-day training seminar to be so extraordinary that they return each year

even though it is not a requirement for those continuing in
the ATI program. ATI focuses on training families for every
area of life and particularly emphasizes parental accountability. The Wisdom Booklets, scripturally based unit studies, are
just one example of the exceptional educational materials
offered by the Institute in Basic Life Principles.

Twenty thousand people attended the ATI conference in
June 1995. Those interested in participating should contact
the institute for further information. Institute in Basic Life
Principles, Advanced Training Institute of America, Box One,
Oak Brook, IL 60522-3001. Telephone: (708) 323-9800.

Legal Services Available to Home Educators

Home School Legal Defense Association
Paeonian Springs, Virginia 22129
703-338-7600

Home School Legal Defense Association was founded in 1983 to bring together a large number of homeschooling families so that each can have a low-cost method of obtaining quality legal defense. HSLDA gives families freedom to homeschool without the fear of facing legal threats alone. The vast majority of the legal threats member-families face are successfully resolved through their early intervention.

Each year thousands of member-families receive legal consultation by letter and phone; each year hundreds more are represented through negotiations with local officials; and dozens are represented in court proceedings. At a cost of one hundred dollars per year, HSLDA provides experienced legal counsel and representation by qualified attorneys to every member family who is challenged in the area of homeschooling. All attorney's fees and costs are paid in full by the association.

The Rutherford Institute
P. O. Box 7482
1445 East Rio Road
Charlottesville, Virginia 22906
804-978-3888

The Rutherford Institute is an international legal and educational organization that specializes in the defense of religious liberty, family rights, and the sanctity of human life and provides legal assistance at no charge to the client. One of the institute's five priority areas is to protect the right to homeschool without improper state intrusion.

Support Organizations for Homeschoolers

National Homeschooling Organizations

(Holt Associates and the Moore Foundation will also help you locate state organizations and local support groups.)

Holt Associates

2269 Massachusetts Ave.
Cambridge, MA 02140
(617) 864-3100

The Moore Foundation

Box 1
Camas, Washington 98607
206-835-5500

   Their low-cost programs are designed to enable students to achieve at the highest levels with the lowest stress, while emphasizing character development. For a complete packet of information about the Moore Academy and Moore Associates, send a fifty-five cent, self-addressed envelope to the Moore Foundation.

National Home Education Research Institute (NHERI)

C/O Western Baptist College
5000 Deer Park Drive SE
Salem, Oregon 97301
503-581-8600

As well as engaging in professional research, NHERI offers print, audio, and video materials in non-technical language. All educators interested in the most current and accurate research findings concerning the resurgence of home education can contact NHERI for information.

National Profamily Organizations

Focus on the Family
James C. Dobson, Ph.D.
Colorado Springs, Colorado   80995
719-531-3400

Family Research Council
Gary L. Bauer, president
700 Thirteenth Street, NW, Suite 500
Washington, D.C.   20005
202-393-2100

Coral Ridge Ministries
Dr. D. James Kennedy
P. O. Box 40
Ft. Lauderdale, Florida   33302
305-772-0404

Eagle Forum
Phyllis Schlafly
Operations Center: P.O. Box 618
Alton, Illinois   62002
618-462-5415

Capitol Hill Office: 316 Pennsylvania Avenue, S.E., Suite 203
Washington, D.C. 20003
202-544-0353

Education Center: 7800 Bonhomme
St. Louis, Missouri 63105
314-721-1213

Concerned Women for America
Beverly LaHaye
370 L'Enfant Promenade SW, Suite 800
Washington, D.C.   20024
202-488-7000

Resources for Homeschool Students

Resources for Homeschooling Special Needs Students

National Challenged Homeschoolers Associated Network (NATTHAN)

5383 Alpine Road S.E.
Olalla, Washington 98359
206-857-4257

NATTHAN membership includes a subscription to their newsletter. They provide information on how to access support networks. They offer an optional family directory. They also produce a resource guide that includes a host of useful material:

Learning in Spite of Labels by Joyce Herzog
Available from Greenleaf Press
615-4499-1617

The Learning Disabled Child: Ways a Parent Can Help by Suzanne Stephens; available from Lifetime Gifts and Books and Bob Jones University Press

National Institute for Learning Disabilities (NILD)

107 Seekel St.
Norfolk, VA 23505-4415
804-423-8646

NILD therapists usually work through Christian schools. Call NILD to find a school closest to you. NILD is based on deficit stimulation and requires one-on-one therapy. It can be expensive, but is very worthwhile.

The Orton Dyslexia Society

724 York Road
Baltimore, MD 23505
301-825-7837

Request the address and phone number of the branch in your state.

Many federal and state agencies provide assistance to special needs students. You should carefully weigh the pros and cons of involving government agencies in your home life. Look in the blue pages under Department of Disabilities and/or Special Needs.

Resources for Homeschooling High School Students

Resource Books for Locating High School Curricula and Courses of Study

The Christian Home Educator's Curriculum Manual by Cathy Duffy

The Big Book of Home Learning: Teen and Adult by Mary Pride

Available from:
Home Life
P.O. Box 1250
Fenton, MO 63026
800-346-6322

Homeschooling the High Schooler, Volumes 1 and 2 by Diana McAlister and Candice Oneschak

High School Your Way by Diana McAlister and Candice Oneschak

Konos has just released its first volume of their high school program: *History of the World Year One: History of the Ancient World.*

For a thorough listing of correspondence courses available for high school students, consult appendix B in Ted Wade's *The Home School Manual.*

For an inspiring book, read *Homeschooling for Excellence* by Micki and David Colfax.

Interactive video and computer programs promise to carry homeschooled high school students into the twenty-first century. Keep your eyes open for these types of products.

> Right now, BJLINC is targeted only to conventional Christian schools. But, eventually this system will be available to homeschoolers via the information superhighway, and students could conceivably go to class from their home computer. ("Coming to You Live, Via Satellite," *The BJU Review*, Summer 1995, 13–15)

(Most of these books can be purchased through Lifetime Books and Gifts.)

Resource Books on College Acceptance and Attendance (At Home or on Campus)

College Admissions: A Guide for Homeschoolers by Judy Gelner

Poppyseed Press
P.O. Box 85
Sedalia, Colorado 80135

The Electronic University: New Educational Alternatives for Students and Adults. This is a Peterson's Guide, available in most secular bookstores.

College Degrees by Mail by Dr. John Bear

Walston's Guide to Earning Religious Degrees Non-Traditionally by Dr. John Bear and Dr. R. Walston

Many colleges offer courses that your high school student can take at home for college credit. A few examples of these are Bob Jones University in Greenville, South Carolina; Taylor University in Fort Wayne, Indiana; and Oral Roberts University in Tulsa, Oklahoma. Call the college of your choice and inquire as to whether they have a program of this nature.

Home School Legal Defense Association keeps a list on file of colleges that have accepted homeschooled students. The list is huge and continues to grow.

Exploring the Apprenticeship Option

Education PLUS+
P.O. Box 1029
Mauldin, SC 29662
803-281-9316

Education PLUS+ offers training materials designed by Ronald and Inge Cannon to assist parents/teachers in working with children and youth. Materials are also available which emphasize parents mentoring their children into adulthood, evaluating college, and exploring apprenticeship options. A free catalogue will be sent upon request.

Distance Learning Resources, Interactive Videos, and Computer Programs

Bob Jones University now offers a distance learning resource to homeschoolers. As of 4 October 1995, six BJLINC classes (course instruction via satellite) will be available for a monthly fee of $89.00. For one fee, families receive all six classes—advanced math, algebra II, physics, biology, chemistry, and Spanish I. Additional classes will be added each year. BJU press has contracted with HomeSat to service home educators with the complete BJLINC courses which are being offered to private schools. A one-time payment of $199 provides for the installation of a twenty-four inch receiving dish in the home and a receiver/decoder box. As part of their service, BJLINC includes a programming guide and a monthly newsletter designed specifically for home educators in a distance learning environment. Homeschool subscribers program their VCRs to record their classes via satellite during the morning hours when satellite time is most affordable. The home educators will be watching classes which are broadcast live via satellite to conventional Christian schools across America. Christian school students interact with BJLINC instructors on a near real-time basis using the satellite and two phone lines going to each classroom. To subscribe or to get more information call Bob Jones University Press toll-free 1-800-739-8199.

Interactive Videos and Computer Programs

Pride's Guide to Educational Software by Bill and Mary Pride, Crossway Books.

Church Bytes Software Guide, A Directory of Software for Church and Christian Home by Neil B. Houk, Church Bytes, Inc., (919) 490-8927. Experts in the area of religious software. Superb annotation.

Video Tutorial Service 1-800-USA-MATH.

Notes

Chapter One

1. Noah Webster, *An American Dictionary of the English Language: Volume 1* (New York: S. Converse, 1828).

2. John Wesley Taylor V, Ph. D., *Home-Based Education: An Alternative That Works* (Rapidan, VA: Hartland Institute), 1.

3. Steven Mintz and Susan Kellogg, *Domestic Revolutions: A Social History of American Family Life* (New York: Free Press, 1988), xiv, quoted by James C. Carper, Ph. D., "Home Schooling, History, and Historians: The Past as Present," *The High School Journal* (Chapel Hill: University of North Carolina Press, 1992), 253–254.

4. James C. Carper, Ph.D., "Home Schooling History and Historians: The Past as Present," *The High School Journal* (Chapel Hill: University of North Carolina Press, 1992) 256.

5. Sam B. Peavey, Ed.D., "Some Observations and Perspectives on Home Education," Prepared for the Iowa State Board of Education (5 August 1989) 1.

6. Ferenc Mate, "Are We Losing Our Children?" *Country Journal* (January/February 1994): 50.

7. Weldon M. Hardenbrook, *Missing from Action: Vanishing Manhood in America* (Nashville: Thomas Nelson Publishers, 1987), 38–39.

8. Cathy Duffy, *Government Nannies* (Gresham, OR: Noble Publishing Associates, 1995), xxiii.

9. Hardenbrook, *Missing from Action*, 96.

10. Ibid., 97.

11. Ansel Adams, *Ansel Adams*, quoted by *Home School Brief* (June 1993): 4.

12. Charles R. Swindoll, *Growing Wise in Family Life* (Portland, OR: Multnomah Press, 1988), 87–106.

13. Dr. Raymond and Dorothy Moore, *The Successful Homeschool Family Handbook* (Nashville: Thomas Nelson Publishers, 1994), 273.

14. Walter B. Barbe, Ph.D., *Growing Up Learning* (Washington, DC: Acropolis Books Ltd., 1985), 15.

15. Ibid., 19–20.

16. A letter received by SCAIHS on 6 January 1995.

Chapter Two

1. "Home Schoolers Score Significantly Above National Average," *Home School Court Report* (Paeonian Springs, VA: Home School Legal Defense Association, 1994), 3.

2. Ibid.

3. *The South Carolina Norm-Referenced Testing Program 1991 Report* (Columbia, SC: South Carolina State Department of Education, 1991).

4. Brian D. Ray, Ph.D., "Home Education Research FACT I SHEET," (Salem, OR: National Home Education Research Institute, 1993).

5. Gary DeMar, *God and Government, Volume I* (Atlanta: American Vision Press, 1982), 8.

6. Ibid.

7. Charles R. Swindoll, *Growing Wise in Family Life* (Portland: Multnomah Press, 1988), 35–36.

8. Richard W. Riley, "Strong Families, Strong Schools," *Vital Speeches of the Day* (1 October 1994): 746.

9. Ibid., 747.

10. Theodore E. Wade, Jr., et. al., *The Home School Manual* (Niles, MI: Gazelle Publications, 1995), 24.

11. Jack H. Grossman, "The Art of Good Teaching," *Sky Magazine* (March 1995): 24–48.

12. Ibid.

13. John 15:13.

14. Sam B. Peavey, Ed. D., "From Observations and Perspectives on Home Education Prepared for the Iowa State Board of Education" (5 August 1989): 2.

15. Swindoll, *Growing Wise in Family Life*, 95.

16. John Wesley Taylor V, Ph.D., *Home-Based Education: An Alternative That Works* (Rapidan, VA: Hartland Institute), 2.

17. Ferenc Mate, "Are We Losing Our Children?" *Country Journal* (Jan./Feb. 1994): 50.

18. Joni and Friends can be contacted at P.O. Box 3333, Agoura, CA, 91301. Phone: 818-707-5664.

19. Riley, "Strong Families, Strong Schools," 747.

20. Charles S. Clark, "Parents and Schools," *The CQ Researcher*, vol. 5, no. 3 (20 January 1995): 51.

21. Keith Geiger, "President's Viewpoint," *NEA Today* (April 1994): 2.

22. Ibid.

Chapter Three

1. Michael P. Farris, *Homeschooling and the Law* (Paeonian Springs, VA: Home School Legal Defense Association, 1990), 8.

2. Ibid., 30.

3. Christopher J. Klicka, *The Right Choice: The Incredible Failure of Public Education and the Rising Hope of Home Schooling* (Gresham, OR: Noble Publishing, 1992), 314,315, 317.

4. Christopher J. Klicka, J. D., *Home Schooling in the United States: A Legal Analysis* (Paeonian Springs, VA: Home School Legal Defense Association, 1994), iii–iv.

5. Farris, *Homeschooling and the Law*, 148.

Chapter Four

1. Luanne Shackelford and Susan White, *A Survivor's Guide to Home Schooling* (Wheaton, IL: Crossway Books, 1988), 3.

2. See appendix D for information on locating local support groups.

3. See appendix D for information on locating state homeschooling organizations.

4. Brian D. Ray, Ph. D., "Home Education Research FACT SHEET III," (Salem, OR: National Home Education Research Institute, 1995).

5. Brian Robertson, "Is Home Schooling in a Class of Its Own?" *Insight* (17 October 1994): 8.

6. Elise Edson, *The SCAIHS High School Handbook* (Columbia, SC: SCAIHS, 1995).

7. For more information on TeenPact and the possibility of bringing it your state, contact Tim Echols at P.O. Box 2111, Norcross, GA, 30091. Phone: 404-256-0634.

Chapter Five

1. *The American Heritage Dictionary of the English Language*, New College Edition, s.v. "socialize."

2. Letter to parents, teachers, and educators from Todd F. Avis, headmaster, Hillsdale Academy, in response to the purchase of the *Hillsdale Academy Reference Guide*, published by Hillsdale College in Hillsdale, Michigan.

3. William J. Bennett, "What To Do About Children," Commentary (March 1995) 25.

4. "Toward Tradition," *Huntington House Notes*, issue 4 (Spring 1995).

5. Norman Cousins, ed., *In God We Trust, The Religious Beliefs and Ideas of the American Founding Fathers* (New York: Harper and Brothers, 1958), 51.

6. Ibid., 50.

7. Ibid., 51.

8. Ibid., 80.

Chapter Six

1. Robert Maynard Hutchins, *The Great Conversation, The Substance of a Liberal Education*, vol. 1 of *Great Books of the Western World* (Chicago: Encyclopedia Britannica, 1952), 2.

2. Ibid., 26.

3. Ibid., xii.

4. Douglas Wilson, "Does History Have a Purpose?" *Practical Homeschooling* (Spring 1995): 14.

5. Hutchins, *Great Books of the Western World*, 71.

6. Ibid., 72.

7. Ibid., xii.

8. Marshall McLuhan, *Understanding Media, The Extensions of Man* (Cambridge, MA: The MIT Press, 1994), 9–21.

9. Mary Hood, Ph.D., *Countdown to Consistency, A Workbook for Home Educators* (self-published, 140 Bond Street Westminster, MD 21157, 1992).

10. *The American Heritage Dictionary*, s.v. "eclecticism."

11. Hutchins, *Great Books of the Western World*, xi.

12. Ibid., xix.

13. Susan Schaffer Macaulay, *For the Children's Sake: Foundations of Education for Home and School* (Westchester, IL: Crossway Books, 1984).

14. *The American Heritage Dictionary*, New College Edition, s.v. "pragmatism."

15. Valerie Bendt, *How to Create Your Own Unit Studies* (Tampa, FL: Common Sense Press, 1994)

16. *The American Heritage Dictionary*, New College Editon, s.v. "existentialism."

17. *Hillsdale Academy Reference Guide* (Hillsdale, MI: Hillsdale College).

18. Ibid.

19. Ibid.

20. Ibid.

21. Ibid.

22. Cynthia Ulrich Tobias, *The Way They Learn, How to Discover and Teach Your Child's Strengths* (Colorado Springs, CO: Focus on the Family Publishing, 1994).

23. *Hillsdale Academy Reference Guide*, page 1 of the Introduction.

24. Ibid.

25. Ibid., page 1 of the Reading List.

Chapter Eight

1. Peter Hubbard, *Sermon Notes*. Numerous sermons delivered by Peter Hubbard dealing with fear of failure, overcoming insecurities, and making ourselves available to God have confirmed the truths the Lord has shown Gary and me. We praise God for His Words to us through the local church. Peter Hubbard is the pastor and teaching elder at North Hills Community Church, Greenville, South Carolina. Peter is finishing a M.Div. at Southern Evangelical Seminary, Charlotte, North Carolina. He holds a B.A. and M.A. from Bob Jones University.

Conclusion

1. Peter Hubbard, *Sermon Notes*.

Anyone Can Homeschool
Seminar and Workshop

For information on their all-day seminar and workshop *Anyone Can Homeschool, How to Find What Works for You,* send a self-addressed stamped envelope to:

Anyone Can Homeschool
P.O. Box 1367
Flat Rock, NC 28731

In the seminar/workshop the authors amplify some of the information discussed in the book, *Anyone Can Homeschool;* they also cover many topics which are not included in the book. The seminar/workshops are conducted on Saturdays during the hours of 9:00 A.M. until 5:00 P.M. Copies of the seminar brochure and the seminar coordinator's guidelines are available on request.

During the seminar/workshop, each speaker presents three workshops—a total of six workshops in all, each examining a different topic. While one of the speakers is conducting a workshop, the other is available in another room for general questions. Therefore, every seminar participant is free to attend all six workshops; or to attend only those of particular interest. The question and answer time with the speakers is an integral part of the seminar/workshop schedule. Resource materials are provided for every workshop.

- How to Build a Support Network

- How to Choose the Right Curriculum

- Public Relations: Dealing Effectively with the Legislature, the Community, and with Public Officials

- How to Teach Reading at Every Age Level; and How to Diagnose Students with Specific Learning Disabilities and Teach Them Effectively

- Teaching Communications Skills K-12: Why Home Is the Best Place to Learn How to Speak, to Write, and to Listen

- How to Homeschool High School Students

We welcome comments from our readers. Feel free to write to us at the following address:

Editorial Department
Huntington House Publishers
P.O. Box 53788
Lafayette, LA 70505

═══════════════════════

More Good Books from Huntington House

The Basic Steps to Successful Homeschooling
by Vicki A. Brady

If you are a parent already convinced of the moral and intellectual benefits of home education, this book is for you. Working on the premise that home education is a wise decision, Vicki Brady, an expert in the field, provides the reader with a practical, nuts-and-bolts approach to implementing a system of home education. Because of its clear, step-by-step format, this book serves as an invaluable guide for beginner and expert alike in the field of home education. The decision to homeschool is a serious, often intimidating one, but one that serves many families well, if carried out properly. This book will make the decision less daunting, providing home educators with a wealth of knowledge and, therefore, confidence.

ISBN 1-56384-113-4

Dinosaurs and the Bible
by David W. Unfred

Every reader, young and old, will be fascinated by this ever-mysterious topic—exactly what happened to the dinosaurs? Author David Unfred draws a very descriptive picture of the history and fate of the dinosaurs, using the Bible as a reference guide. Did dinosaurs really exist? Does the Bible mention dinosaurs? What happened to dinosaurs, or are there some still living, awaiting discovery?

ISBN Hardcover 0-910311-70-6

High on Adventure:
Stories of Good, Clean,
Spine-tingling Fun
by Stephen Arrington

From meeting a seventeen-and-a-half-foot great white shark face to face, to diving from an airplane toward the earth's surface at 140 M.P.H., to exploring a sunken battle cruiser from World War II in the dark depths of the South Pacific Ocean, author and adventurer Stephen Arrington retells many exciting tales from his life as a navy frogman and chief diver for the Cousteau Society. Each story is laced with Arrington's Christian belief and outlook that life is an adventure waiting to be had.

ISBN 1-56384-082-0

Conquering the Culture:
The Fight for Our Children's Souls
by David Paul Eich

Remember Uncle Screwtape? He was the charming C.S. Lewis character who tried to educate his nephew, Wormwood, on the art of destroying souls. Now, from a fictional town in Montana, comes a similar allegory. This compelling book is a valuable source of support for parents who need both answers and courage to raise moral children in an immoral world.

ISBN 1-56384-101-0

Out of Control—
Who's Watching Our Child
Protection Agencies?
by Brenda Scott

This book of horror stories is true. The deplorable and unauthorized might of Child Protection Services is capable of reaching into and destroying any home in America. No matter how innocent and happy your family may be, you are one accusation away from disaster. Social workers are allowed to violate constitutional rights and often become judge, jury, and executioner. Innocent parents may appear on computer registers and be branded "child abuser" for life. Every year, it is estimated that over 1 million people are falsely accused of child abuse in this country. You could be next, says author and speaker Brenda Scott.

ISBN 1-56384-069-3

Children No More:
How We Lost a Generation
by Brenda Scott

Child abuse, school yard crime, gang-land murders, popular lyrics laced with death motifs, twisted couplings posing as love on MTV and day-time soap operas (both accessible by latch-key children), loving parents portrayed as the enemy, condom pushers, drug apologists, philandering leaders . . . is it any wonder heroes and role models are passe? The author grieves the loss of a generation but savors a hope that the next can be saved.

ISBN 1-56384-083-9

Order These Huntington House Books

- *Anyone Can Homeschool*—Terry Dorian, Ph.D. & Zan Peters Tyler
- *The Assault*—Dale A. Berryhill
- *Beyond Political Correctness*—Dr. David Thibodaux
- *The Best of HUMAN EVENTS*—Edited by James C. Roberts
- *Bleeding Hearts and Propaganda*—James R. Spencer
- *Can Families Survive in Pagan America?*—Samuel Dresner
- *Circle of Death*—Richmond Odom
- *Children No More*—Brenda Scott
- *Combat Ready*—Lynn Stanley
- *The Compassionate Conservative*—Joseph J. Jacobs, Ph.D.
- *Conservative, American & Jewish*—Jacob Neusner, Ph.D.
- *The Culture War in America*—Bob Rosio
- *The Dark Side of Freemasonry*—Ed Decker
- *The Demonic Roots of Globalism*—Gary Kah
- *Do Angels Really Exist?*—Dr. David O. Dykes
- *En Route to Global Occupation*—Gary Kah
- *Everyday Evangelism*—Ray Comfort
- **Exposing the AIDS Scandal*—Dr. Paul Cameron
- *Freud's War with God*—Jack Wright, Jr., Ph.D.
- *Global Bondage*—Cliff Kincaid
- *Goddess Earth*—Samantha Smith
- *Health Begins in Him*—Terry Dorian, Ph.D.
- *Heresy Hunters*—Jim Spencer
- *Hidden Dangers of the Rainbow*—Constance Cumbey
- *High-Voltage Christianity*—Michael Brown
- *High on Adventure*—Stephen Arrington
- *How to Homeschool (Yes, You!)*—Julia Toto
- *Hungry for God*—Larry E. Myers
- *I Shot an Elephant in My Pajamas*—Morrie Ryskind w/ John Roberts
- **Inside the New Age Nightmare*—Randall Baer
- *A Jewish Conservative Looks at Pagan America*—Don Feder
- *Journey into Darkness*—Stephen Arrington
- *Kinsey, Sex and Fraud*—Dr. Judith A. Reisman & Edward Eichel
- *The Liberal Contradiction*—Dale A. Berryhill
- *The Media Hates Conservatives*—Dale A. Berryhill
- *New Gods for a New Age*—Richmond Odom
- *One Man, One Woman, One Lifetime*—Rabbi Reuven Bulka
- *Out of Control*—Brenda Scott
- *Outcome-Based Education*—Peg Luksik & Pamela Hoffecker
- *Please Tell Me*—Tom McKenney
- *Revival: Its Principles and Personalities*—Winkie Pratney
- *The Truth about False Memory Syndrome*—James Friesen, Ph.D.

*Available in Salt Series

Available at bookstores everywhere or order direct from:
Huntington House Publishers • P.O. Box 53788 • Lafayette, LA 70505

Call toll-free 1-800-749-4009.